Mark A. Wrathall is Associate Professor of Philosophy at Brigham Young University. He has edited or co-edited a number of volumes on Heidegger's thought, including *Heidegger Reexamined; Appropriating Heidegger; Heidegger, Coping and Cognitive Science; Heidegger, Authenticity and Modernity;* and *A Companion to Heidegger.*

HOW TO READ

HOW
TO
READ

HEIDEGGER

MARK WRATHALL

W. W. Norton & Company
New York   London

First published in Great Britain by Granta Publications

Being and Time by Martin Heidegger, trans. John Macquarie and Edward
Robinson, SCM Press 1962; reprinted with the permission of the publisher.
Basic Writings, revised and expanded edn, by Martin Heidegger, ed. David
Farrell Krell; English translation © 1977, 1993, by HarperCollins Publishers
Inc.; general introduction and introductions to each selection copyright ©
1977, 1993, by David Farrell Krell; reprinted by permission of HarperCollins
Publishers Inc. *The Question Concerning Technology and Other Essays* by Martin
Heidegger, trans. William Lovitt, English language translation © 1977 by
Harper & Row Publishers Inc.; reprinted by permission of HarperCollins
Publishers Inc.; *Poetry, Language, Thought* by Martin Heidegger, trans. and
with an introduction by Albert Hofstadter; copyright © 1971 by Martin
Heidegger; reprinted by permission of HarperCollins Publishers Inc.

For information about permission to reproduce selections from this book,
write to Permissions, W. W. Norton & Company, Inc.,
500 Fifth Avenue, New York, NY 10110

Manufacturing by The Maple-Vail Book Manufacturing Group
Production manager: Amanda Morrison

Library of Congress Cataloging-in-Publication Data

Wrathall, Mark A.
How to read Heidegger / Mark Wrathall. — 1st American ed.
p. cm. — (How to read)
Includes bibliographical references and index.
ISBN-13: 978-0-393-32880-6 (pbk.)
ISBN-10: 0-393-32880-5 (pbk.)
1. Heidegger, Martin, 1889–1976. I. Title. II. Series: How to
read (New York, N.Y.)
B3279.H49W73 2006
193—dc22
2005035276

W. W. Norton & Company, Inc., 500 Fifth Avenue, New York, N.Y. 10110
www.wwnorton.com

W. W. Norton & Company Ltd.
Castle House, 75/76 Wells Street, London W1T 3QT

1 2 3 4 5 6 7 8 9 0

CONTENTS

SERIES EDITOR'S FOREWORD

How am I to read *How to Read*?

This series is based on a very simple, but novel idea. Most beginners' guides to great thinkers and writers offer either potted biography or condensed summaries of their major works, or perhaps even both. *How to Read*, by contrast, brings the reader face-to-face with the writing itself in the company of an expert guide. Its starting point is that in order to get close to what a writer is all about, you have to get close to the words they actually use and be shown how to read those words.

Every book in the series is in a way a masterclass in reading. Each author has selected ten or so short extracts from a writer's work and looks at them in detail as a way of revealing their central ideas and thereby opening doors onto a whole world of thought. Sometimes these extracts are arranged chronologically to give a sense of a thinker's development over time, sometimes not. The books are not merely compilations of a thinker's most famous passages, their 'greatest hits', but rather they offer a series of clues or keys that will enable readers to go on and make discoveries of their own. In addition to the texts and readings, each book provides a short biographical chronology and suggestions for further reading, Internet resources, and so on. The books in the *How to Read* series don't claim to tell you all you need to know about Freud, Nietzsche and Darwin, or indeed Shakespeare and the Marquis de Sade, but they do offer the best starting point for further exploration.

Unlike the available second-hand versions of the minds that have shaped our intellectual, cultural, religious, political and scientific landscape, *How to Read* offers a refreshing set of first-hand encounters with those minds. Our hope is that these books will, by turn, instruct, intrigue, embolden, encourage and delight.

Simon Critchley
New School for Social Research, New York

ACKNOWLEDGEMENTS

I am indebted to the many friends and colleagues who have read this book and made suggestions for improvement, or have discussed matters of interpretation and translation with me. I would like to acknowledge especially the contributions of Hubert Dreyfus, James Faulconer, Ariane Uhlin, Jeffrey Johnson and James Olsen.

INTRODUCTION

In Heidegger's case, the question of how to read him may be of less immediate interest than the question 'Why read Heidegger?' Of those who have heard something about him, many dismiss him as an unrepentant ex-Nazi, pompous and mystical, more sophist than philosopher, anti-modernist and irrationalist, given to asking obscure questions like 'What is being?' or 'What is the nothing?', and to offering even more obscure answers like 'Being is not', or 'the nothing noths'.

And yet, Heidegger was one of the most important thinkers of the twentieth century. One could measure his significance by the number and variety of other important philosophers who have been profoundly influenced by his work – they include German philosophers like Hannah Arendt, Hans-Georg Gadamer, and Jürgen Habermas, French philosophers like Jean-Paul Sartre, Simone de Beauvoir, Maurice Merleau-Ponty, Michel Foucault and Jacques Derrida, and philosophers in the English-speaking tradition like Charles Taylor, Richard Rorty, Hubert Dreyfus and Stanley Cavell. Or, one could assess his importance by the number of fields which have been shaped by his work: theorists in fields as diverse as theology, anthropology, sociology, psychology, political science and the humanities have turned to Heidegger for inspiration.

For those influenced by Heidegger, it is not his misadventures with Naziism or his self-importance that is paramount in interpreting his philosophy, but his originality as a thinker and the scope and profundity of his thought itself. For them, Heidegger's work, as difficult as it is to understand, cuts through centuries if not millennia of philosophical errors, and addresses the central topics of human existence – truth, language, human nature and the foundations of knowledge.

In some ways, the controversy over Heidegger is symptomatic of philosophy's identity crisis in the English-speaking world – a crisis over the proper role and aspirations of philosophy. With the successes and accompanying prestige of the natural sciences in modern times, philosophy has been displaced as the 'noblest pursuit of all' (Plato, *Republic* 489c). Analytical philosophers (who, by and large, are dismissive of Heidegger's work) have typically adopted a humble view of the role of philosophy. For them, philosophy has to make a choice: either it becomes a historical study of past philosophical positions, or it can become an adjunct to the empirical sciences, by engaging in conceptual and linguistic analysis. Thus, philosophy could assist science by clarifying its concepts, sorting out its theoretical confusions, perhaps making us more aware of limitations in the ways in which we represent the world in thought and language. Philosophers with analytical sensibilities often see Heidegger as a throwback to the bad old days of metaphysical (i.e., unscientific) speculation – an appearance only heightened by his seeming inability or refusal to make clear, logical, analytical arguments. That Heidegger was a member of the Nazi Party only makes it that much easier for analytical philosophers to ignore him or dismiss him with a footnote. John Searle accurately summed up the analytical reaction to Heidegger when he noted: 'Most philosophers in the Anglo-American tradition seem to think that Heidegger was an obscurantist muddle-head at best or an unregenerate Nazi at worst' (Searle, p. 71).

From the analytical perspective, philosophy risks disaster

whenever it takes on the big questions about the purpose of life and the nature of reality. As a result, analytical philosophy rarely tackles such topics. The positive reception of Heidegger in the English-speaking world was shaped early on by the impression that his work repudiated the pre-eminence of the empirical sciences and reclaimed the noble standing of philosophy. Werner Brock, who first published a translation of Heidegger's work into English, summarized this view (oft repeated in early English-language articles on Heidegger) in lectures at the University of London in 1935:

> Heidegger's purpose in *Being and Time* . . . is to show that, far from having reached the end of philosophical enquiry, . . . we have hardly come in sight of the most fundamental problems which must be attacked, and that these problems must be attacked, not by science, which concerns itself with limited spheres of existence, but only by the philosophers of the future . . . With this thematic task, which in its universality transcends all other endeavours of contemporary academic philosophy, Heidegger attempts to raise philosophy again to a height which in the nineteenth century, the age of science, it seemed to have lost forever. (Brock, pp. 116–17)

In the contemporary philosophical scene, many share Brock's view of Heidegger as an opponent to the humble and deflated vision of philosophy endorsed by analytical philosophers.

There is a philosophical movement – so-called 'continental philosophy' – which sees itself as an antagonist to analytical philosophy, and views Heidegger as a champion in the struggle to restore philosophy to its former grandeur. Continental philosophers by and large see analytical philosophy as consigning itself to irrelevance by relinquishing the grand problems of philosophy in favour of pedantic and scholastic inquiry into the functioning of language. Heidegger, continental philosophers believe, shows that analytical philosophy's adjunct position vis-à-vis the sciences amounts to a kind of philosophical naivete – an uncritical faith in scientific naturalism and philosophical logic as ways to access ultimate reality.

The initial impression of Heidegger as a champion of antiscientific and speculative philosophy, an impression fostered by Brock and many others, quickly developed into a picture that, in a funny way, supports both the analytical dismissal of, and the continental attachment to, Heidegger. Marjorie Glicksman summarized the analyst's uneasiness with Heidegger in a critical review of his philosophy published in 1938:

> These, then, are some of the elements in Heidegger's philosophy: the repudiation of traditional philosophy in any but a radically novel interpretation, the rejection of the scientific attitude, the immersion in phenomena, the consequent baptism of these phenomena with new tongue-twisting titles, and the construction on their base of towers of mystifying dogmata; the founding of such systems, finally, upon plausible descriptions of psychological and epistemological phenomena and reasonable generalizations about experience. (Glicksman, p. 104)

A key feature of Heidegger's method, Glicksman further observed, was the practice of 'forestall[ing] any interventions that might arise from science, logic, or common sense' (ibid., p. 97). With the exception of the desultory phrase 'mystifying dogmata', Glicksman's description of Heidegger's philosophy and method could have been written by any number of Heidegger's supporters, and remains surprisingly contemporary, despite the subsequent publication and translation of works that should have called the picture into question. The result is that, to many 'continental philosophers', any effort to make Heidegger's thought clearer, to recover its argumentative structure, to see it as engaged in the philosophical disputes over language and mind that have animated twentieth-century analytical philosophy – any such efforts are viewed as a betrayal of Heidegger's radicality as a thinker and his revolutionary effort to overcome the impasses of modern philosophy.

To my mind, the most important development in Heidegger's reception in the English-speaking world is the growing recognition that this picture of Heidegger is a caricature – it contains, to be sure, a kernel of truth. But it also distorts a great deal, and does so in a way that hardens the spurious opposition between analytical rigour of thought and continental relevance to lived experience. It does this by misunderstanding the true significance of Heidegger's resistance to natural scientific categories, his use of phenomenological descriptions, and the consequent place of logical argumentation in his work. This development has taken hold as philosophers trained in the analytical tradition of thought have turned to Heidegger's philosophy, and discovered that it contains a wealth of insight into the limitations of certain traditional views of human existence, 'mind', the nature of language, and so on – traditional views that analytical philosophers, too, have struggled to overcome. At the same time, philosophers trained in the continental tradition have discovered that analytical philosophy is neither as sterile nor as irrelevant to the 'big questions' of life as one might suppose, and that many analytical philosophers are engaged in projects that parallel Heidegger's own efforts to rethink the nature of human existence and our place in the world.

What is Heidegger's contribution to thinking? Why, despite the challenges posed by his difficult and unconventional prose (the common picture of Heidegger was not wrong about *that*), is he worth our striving to understand? Heidegger did more than any other thinker of the twentieth century to develop a coherent way of thinking and talking about human existence without reducing it to a natural scientific phenomenon or treating it as a ghostly mind haunting the physical world. This has inspired artists and social scientists, who have struggled to acknowledge the dignity and freedom of human existence; it has inspired scientists who have tried to keep mindful of the limits of scientific inquiry; and it has challenged us all to rethink our place in history and the direction in which we as a scientific and technological culture are moving.

1

DASEIN AND BEING-IN-THE-WORLD

Dasein is an entity which, in its very being, comports itself understandingly towards that being. In saying this, we are calling attention to the formal concept of existence. Dasein exists. Furthermore, Dasein is an entity which in each case I myself am. Mineness belongs to any existent Dasein, and belongs to it as the condition which makes authenticity and inauthenticity possible . . .

But these are both ways in which Dasein's being takes on a definite character, and they must be seen and understood *a priori* as grounded upon that state of being which we have called 'being-in-the-world'. An interpretation of this constitutive state is needed if we are to set up our analytic of Dasein correctly. The compound expression 'being-in-the-world' indicates in the very way we have coined it, that it stands for a *unitary* phenomenon. This primary datum must be seen as a whole. But while being-in-the-world cannot be broken up into contents which may be pieced together, this does not prevent it from having several constitutive items in its structure. (*Being and Time*, p. 78)

Heidegger's dense style and free use of philosophical terms (some would say 'jargon') can make reading *Being and Time* a frustrating experience for a beginner. The passage above is typical in that it uses several terms in ways unique to Heidegger. Indeed, the first sentence alone contains terms either unfamiliar to those uninitiated in 'Heideggerese', or ordinary terms used in a technical and unfamiliar sense: 'entity', 'being', 'comport' and 'Dasein'. Many readers in the English-speaking world have never got beyond their initial frustration. It has led many to reject Heidegger's work as obfuscatory and mystical. I think this is a mistake – Heidegger rewards the patient reader with genuine insight. Much of the difficulty comes from the fact that Heidegger is trying to do something that our ordinary language is not designed to do – talk about the most fundamental features of our existence. Ordinary language is very good at talking about ordinary objects, events and experiences. Poets often need to subject our ordinary language to considerable strain to express extraordinary experiences, and even then we are left with the feeling that there are some things that just cannot be said in words. Heidegger viewed his task as a philosopher as very similar to that of the poet, and he was willing to torture the German language to help us understand experiences and things that cannot really be captured in words and concepts. The English-speaking reader has an additional disadvantage of reading Heidegger through the eyes of translators who have not always understood his meaning, and in translations which do not always use the most natural and straightforward way to render his thoughts into English. I will, from time to time, correct or alter the translations to make them clearer.

As Heidegger himself taught, all understanding moves in a circle. We use an author's description to lead us to the subject under discussion, and we use our own apprehension of that subject as the clue to deciphering the author's description. As we move back and forth between the description and the thing described, our understanding of both is enriched. That is precisely how one must read Heidegger – let his descriptions teach you how to see things even as you let the things themselves guide your interpretation of his terms. Heidegger's philosophical 'method', such as it is, consists in resolving philosophical problems by describing the phenomenon at the root of the problem in such a way that it can be seen free of any distortion. 'Phenomenon' is, of course, more philosophical jargon. In its most basic and broadest sense, it means simply 'that which shows itself from itself' (see *Being and Time*, p. 51). As I walk through a park, I see trees and benches and dogs and other people. Each of them is a phenomenon, something I can experience. According to physicists, those trees and benches and dogs are composed of atoms and molecules; biologists tell me that the trees and dogs and people are constituted by their DNA; psychologists and philosophers tell me that the essence of people is found in their minds. But atoms, DNA and minds don't show themselves as I walk through the park. They might announce themselves through the things that do appear, but I do not directly experience them.

'"Phenomenology" means,' Heidegger said, 'to let that which shows itself be seen from itself in the very way in which it shows itself from itself' (*Being and Time*, p. 58). Phenomenology requires us to stick with the things that appear in experience, and learn to see them in such a way that they show up as they really are. When a physicist tries to persuade you that what you *really* see are light waves bouncing off the reflective surfaces of physical bodies, her argument is unphenomenological. She is confusing two different things – one is the causal interaction of our bodies and objects in the world, the other is what it is actually like to experience the world. The physicist's account thus strays from what you actually experience directly – park benches and people – and tries to reconstruct that experience in foreign terms. Because it confuses two different kinds of things – experiences and causes – this reconstruction ends up actually creating more problems than it solves. Psychologists and philosophers have struggled in vain to explain how light waves bouncing around can get converted into an experience of a park bench. Phenomenologists believe that a clear view of the phenomena will usually dissolve these kinds of problems more effectively than any philosophical argument can. We never see light waves, nor do we see the pattern the light waves project onto our retinas. That means that we never have to transform light waves and optical projections into park benches and people.

In the extract above, Heidegger offers a phenomenological description of the entity that each of us is. In trying to understand his description, you should make constant reference to your own experience of being who you are. Let Heidegger's description guide your reflection on what it is like to be a person. But you should be critical as well – check his description against your own experience.

One of Heidegger's most innovative and important insights is that human existence is grounded in our always already finding ourselves in a world. A 'mind' as traditionally conceived can exist without a world. According to the tradition that started with Descartes (1596–1650), the entire world could be one grand illusion, and still the mind could go on thinking its thoughts and feeling its feelings. Heidegger, to the contrary, argues that having thoughts and feelings is only possible for an entity who is actively engaged in the world, and he dedicates a considerable portion of *Being and Time* to a detailed phenomenological description of what is involved in being in a world. On the basis of this description, he argues that the philosophical tradition has overlooked the true character of the world, and the nature of our human existence in a world. He calls the kind of entity that we humans are 'Dasein'.

The first translators of Heidegger left the term 'Dasein' untranslated,[1] and this practice has been followed ever since. In fact, use of 'Dasein' is so common now in English-language texts inspired by Heidegger that it has its own entry in the *Oxford English Dictionary*. Taken literally, *Dasein* means being-there (from the German *Da*, 'there', and *Sein*, 'being'). In colloquial German, '*Dasein*' means 'existence', but Heidegger uses it specifically to refer to entities like us. He is not saying that humans *have* Dasein, he is saying that we each *are* a Dasein. We are a Dasein because of the way we exist in the world. Heidegger deliberately chose the term because of its literal connotations – Dasein always has a 'there', a place in which it understands how to comport itself, and within which it has meaningful relationships to other entities. No other philosophical name for human beings – names like 'subject' or 'rational animal' – is quite so good at capturing what Heidegger thinks is distinctive about us: that we always find ourselves surrounded by particular objects and items of equipment, and caught up in particular activities and goals, all of which contribute to making up a particular situation.

The first sentence of our extract says: 'Dasein is an entity which, in its very being, comports itself understandingly towards that being.' 'To comport' means to behave oneself or carry oneself. We might say that she comported herself bravely in battle, or that he comported himself poorly at the office party, but we do not usually say that someone 'comports herself towards' something.[2] Heidegger's turn of phrase shows us that every particular action or thought grows out of a style or way of carrying ourselves. If I insult my boss at the office party, this action has its roots in my bad or insensitive comportment. By the same token, every way of comporting or carrying ourselves involves acting with respect to particular things or people. The one who comports herself bravely only does so in so far as she does something *to* something – for instance, she fights resolutely against the enemy. Dasein's most basic and essential comportment is a comportment towards being. That means that very particular thing a Dasein does grows out of a certain style or manner of existing in the world and, in acting, Dasein relates itself to that understanding of its being. This ultimately means, as we shall see, that Daseins, unlike other entities, are capable of taking responsibility for the way they exist in the world.

'The being of something is that on the basis of which it is the thing that it is.' Nowadays, we tend to recognize only one way or mode of being: the being of physical entities. What a thing *really* is, we assume, is a matter of its physical make-up. A lump of dirt *is* a lump of dirt because of the physical properties it possesses. These are the properties that can be measured using scientific instruments – mass, the wavelength of light reflected by the dirt (that is, colour), solubility in water, chemical reactivity and so on. To be a lump of dirt is to have just those physical properties. Thus, the being of the lump of dirt is determined by physicality. In fact, we tend to think that almost everything has the same mode of being. (Park benches are *really* just material entities arranged in a particular way. Even people are *really* just a certain kind of biological organism.)

Heidegger, by contrast, believed in a multiplicity of ways of being; physicality or 'substantiality', according to Heidegger, is just one of the modes of being (see *Being and Time*, pp. 122–5). In addition, Heidegger argued that Dasein and meaningful objects (like park benches and hammers) have ways of being that cannot be reduced to possessing physical properties. Meaningful objects have, as their mode of being, involvement with other meaningful things. A hammer is what it is in virtue of its relationship to things like nails and boards, and its use in activities like hammering. In later works, Heidegger considered other modes of being like that of animal life and works of art.

One key feature of Dasein's being – one of the things which makes us the kind of entities we are – is that we understand our being and thus are able to comport ourselves towards it. This distinguishes Dasein from most natural entities (rocks, trees, scorpions, electrons, etc.) as well as from most artefacts (houses, computers, stock markets, etc.). Those kinds of things don't understand their being, and they therefore are not capable of doing anything to their way of being. When a tree grows, it neither reaffirms nor calls into question its being as a living thing – it just is what it is. But everything we do either reinforces or undermines the way we live in the world.

Heidegger names Dasein's way of being in the second and third sentences of our passage: 'In saying this, we are calling attention to the formal concept of existence (*Existenz*). Dasein exists (*existiert*).' Heidegger is using the word 'exist' in a technical manner; non-Daseinish things (things like snowflakes and speedboats) do not 'exist', but that does not mean that there are no such things. Instead, it means they have a different mode of being. Something only 'exists' in Heidegger's sense when its way of being is one particular interpretation of how it should be the thing it is. This notion of existence had a profound influence on the French existentialist movement, and was a direct inspiration for Sartre's slogan 'existence precedes essence'. This slogan was Sartre's way of expressing the idea that there is no absolute, unchanging, ideal way to be human.[3]

Existence is described by Heidegger as Dasein's possibility 'to be itself or not itself' (*Being and Time*, p. 33). Because I don't *have* to live the way I do, it follows that I am ultimately responsible for who I am or how I live. The question is whether I will be myself – whether I will own up to the responsibility for being who I am. Thus, as Heidegger notes in the excerpt above, a fundamental trait of Dasein is 'mineness', my being belongs to me; who I am is my trait, and nobody else's.

Heidegger's name for the kind of existence in which we take responsibility for our being is 'authenticity' or *Eigentlichkeit*, which comes from *eigen*, the adjective for what is one's own or proper. *Eigentlich* means real or proper, so the authentic Dasein is the one who has become its own, that is, become an individual, and in so doing realized what is most proper to it as a Dasein – namely, owning up to its 'mineness', to its ability to decide for itself on its own being. The inauthentic Dasein, by contrast, has not taken responsibility for itself, but lives in the way that others think it should. Indeed, there is a tendency, Heidegger believes, to cede to others the power to decide who and how one should be. Responsibility is a frightening thing. But even inauthentic being, in which Dasein 'is not itself', is something for which Dasein is responsible. If I am inauthentic, my inauthentic being is still mine.

Here again, Sartre and the French existentialists were deeply influenced by Heidegger. Sartre captured this idea of our inescapable responsibility with another one of his famous slogans: 'We are condemned to be free.' But Heidegger would take issue with Sartre's way of expressing the idea, because it doesn't fully appreciate the limits of our responsibility. Sartre, in some ways, remains tied to the subjectivist tradition that starts with Descartes. According to Descartes, we are not fundamentally being-in-the-world, we are subjects – beings with mental states and experiences which can be what they are independently of the state of the surrounding world. Descartes puts the point this way: 'I [am] a substance the whole essence or nature of which [is] merely to think, and which, in order to exist, need[s] no place and depend[s] on no material thing' (*Discourse on Method*, p. 18). In this view, who I am is independent of the actual, concrete relationships in which I find myself involved. In this kind of subjectivist view, Sartre's radical freedom makes sense – I can change who I am simply by changing how I think about things.

For Heidegger, by contrast, our way of being is found not in our thinking nature, but in our existing in a place with particular things and established ways of doing things. Our existence means that we can take responsibility for what we do. But it doesn't mean that we are free to ignore the limits on being that the world sets. The world offers to Dasein a specific range of ways in which it can be. It opens up a variety of possibilities (like being a musician or a metallurgist); it provides a variety of different tools for pursuing those possibilities (like oboes and guitars and drums); and it establishes styles and norms of behaviour. The world thus gives us a domain in which we are set free to act, but also gives us standards to which we can simply submit.

Dasein's ability to take a stand on its being is grounded in the fact that, in its very being, Dasein comports itself in a world and relates itself to other entities. The kind of being we have, the way we carry ourselves and live our lives, is intimately and inextricably bound up with the state of the world that we find ourselves in. A musician's ability to devote her life to music, for example, depends on and is shaped by the fact that, in our world, there are already existing kinds of musical instruments, musical practices, institutions for the performance, recording and dissemination of music, as well as lots of non-musical institutions, objects and practices. Because our society requires payment for food and housing, for example, a musician's ability to pursue her art will be impacted by everyday needs and demands. Because Dasein doesn't have any fixed way it must be, what it *is* will always be a complex product of the decisions it makes, the skills and habits and practices it fosters, and the objects, institutions and other worldly structures within which it finds itself. Heidegger concludes in our passage above that Dasein is not a subject, self-constituted independently of the objects and world around it. Dasein is most fundamentally a 'being-in-the-world'. Heidegger hyphenates the word to 'indicate in the very way we have coined it that it stands for a unitary phenomenon. This primary datum must be seen as a whole.' There can't be a Dasein without a world, in other words, nor a world without Dasein. And what Dasein *is* can only be read off the world as it acts in the world.

2

THE WORLD

To Dasein's being, an understanding of being belongs. Any understanding [*Verständnis*] has its being in an act of understanding [*Verstehen*]. If being-in-the-world is a kind of being which is essentially befitting to Dasein, then to understand being-in-the-world belongs to the essential content of its understanding of being. The previous disclosure of that for which what we encounter within-the-world is subsequently freed, amounts to nothing else than understanding the world – that world towards which Dasein as an entity always comports itself.

Whenever we let there be an involvement with something in something beforehand, our doing so is grounded in our understanding such things as letting something be involved, and such things as the 'with-which' and the 'in-which' of involvements. Anything of this sort, and anything else that is basic for it, such as the 'towards-this', as that in which there is an involvement, or such as the 'for-the-sake-of-which' to which every 'towards-which' ultimately goes back – all these must be disclosed beforehand with a certain intelligibility [*Verständlichkeit*]. And what is that wherein Dasein as being-in-the-world understands itself pre-ontologically? In understanding a context of relations such as we have mentioned, Dasein has assigned itself to an 'in-order-to' [*Um-zu*], and it has done so in terms of a potentiality-for-being for the sake of which it itself is – one which it may have seized upon either explicitly or tacitly, and which may be either authentic or inauthentic. This 'in-order-to' prescribes a 'towards-this' as a possible 'in-which' for letting something be involved; and the structure of letting it be involved implies that this is an involvement which something *has* – an involvement which is *with* something. Dasein always assigns itself from a 'for-the-sake-of-which' to the 'with-which' of an involvement; that is to say, to the extent that it is, it always lets entities be encountered as ready-to-hand. *That wherein* [*Worin*] Dasein understands itself beforehand in the mode of assigning itself is *that for which* [*das Woraufhin*] it has let entities be encountered beforehand. *The 'wherein' of an act of understanding which assigns or refers itself, is that for which one lets entities be encountered in the kind of being that belongs to involvements; and this 'wherein' is the phenomenon of the world.* And the structure of that to which Dasein assigns itself is what makes up the *worldhood* of the world.

That wherein Dasein already understands itself in this way is always something with which it is primordially familiar. This familiarity with the world does not necessarily require that the relations which are constitutive for the world as world should be theoretically transparent. (*Being and Time*, pp. 118–19)

The modern scientific study of the world is built on the ideal of a scientific method – a methodological and objective way of gathering facts and formulating theories. The emphasis on method is based on a fact that strikes us moderns as obvious: our everyday understanding of things may very well conceal the true functioning of nature. What could be more apparent than that the sun rises in the morning, moves across the sky, and sets in the west in the evening? And yet the truth of the matter is that our senses are deceiving us – we are the ones who are moving around the sun.

Science only began to uncover the laws that govern the natural order when it learned methodically to disregard the world as it makes sense to us, the world as it appears in our natural, everyday dealings with things. As Francis Bacon argued in 1620, the progress of science requires that we first clear away 'the idols and false notions which are now in possession of the human understanding, and have taken deep root therein, [and] so beset men's minds that truth can hardly find entrance' (*New Organon*, XXXVIII). The first 'idol' that Bacon tackled was the 'false assertion that the sense of man is the measure of things. On the contrary, all perceptions as well of the sense as of the mind are according to the measure of the individual and not according to the measure of the universe. And the human understanding is like a false mirror, which, receiving rays irregularly, distorts and discolours the nature of things by mingling its own nature with it' (*New Organon*, XLI). To establish science on a sound footing, then, it was necessary to develop a method for filtering out the subjective distortions that we inevitably impose on the world.

Science has in large part heeded Bacon's advice. Scientists discipline themselves to ignore our human way of making sense of things, of relating things to each other, of feeling about or valuing things, and try instead to approach things neutrally. Their aim is to isolate just those properties of things which are causally efficacious. The results have been so impressive that we now are ready to concede that the values we 'give' to things and the meanings we 'attach' to things may not *really* be in the world at all. J. L. Mackie could thus plausibly insist that 'there are no objective values', that things like moral goodness, duty, obligation, beauty, etc. 'are not part of the fabric of the world' (*Ethics*, p. 15). There is, after all, no scientific way to resolve disputes over values, to decide, for example, whether a painting really has aesthetic merit or not. Such valuations therefore seem to be a kind of projection – in Bacon's words, a 'distortion and discolouring of the nature of things' – that we impose on a meaningless and indifferent universe. The world we inhabit is *actually* nothing but a collection of physical objects.

Or is it? Does the success of the sciences in explaining and modelling the behaviour of the physical universe really support the conclusion that all the meanings we find in the world are a kind of subjective projection? To reach this conclusion, Heidegger argues, is to confuse the universe with the world (see *The Basic Problems of Phenomenology*, p. 165). The physical universe, he is willing to grant, is best explored through the natural sciences. In this day and age, no one could really believe that we could discover the nature of physical reality – for example, the properties of electrons and quarks and the such – by exploring our everyday understanding of things. But there is a legitimate sense in which we use the word 'world' to name something quite different, something like a particular style of organizing our activities and relations with the things and people around us. The world understood in this way simply doesn't lend itself to be studied using the methodology of the physical sciences. Instead, we only understand a world by somehow finding a way into it and the experience of the things it gives birth to. Whole books are devoted to helping us get a feel for foreign worlds – *The World of the Reformation* or *The World of Texas Politics*, or *The World of the Maya* or *The World of the Suicide Bomber*. Despite the fact that the very same physical and chemical laws apply to both Texas politicians and suicide bombers, there is a very real sense in which they inhabit different worlds.

Heidegger thinks that the world, understood in this sense,

is a genuine phenomenon in its own right, and can't be reduced to a mere collection of physical objects. A world that we understand, that makes sense to us, that gives structure to and organizes all the things we encounter in our everyday lives – such a world makes it possible for us to act on, think about and experience things in the world. As the extract above indicates, Heidegger believes that it is an essential feature of Dasein (the kind of being we are) that it understands the world, and that it is always comporting itself towards the world. If, swayed by the success of the physical sciences, we insist that what *really* exists are brute physical objects, then we will fail to recognize how everything we do is shaped by a world. And that means we will ultimately fail to understand ourselves.

So what is the world, if it is not a physical entity? How does the world shape the things that we encounter and the activities we perform? And what does it mean to understand the world? The passage above begins with the claim that an essential feature of Dasein's being, of what it is to be Dasein, is having an understanding of the world. That means that something only is a Dasein provided that it understands how to 'comport itself towards the world'. We sometimes think that our understanding consists in knowing particular facts or propositions. If that were what Heidegger had in mind here, then his claim would be that every Dasein, in addition to knowing some facts about particular objects, also knew facts about its world. Then we could understand, for example, the world of the suicide bomber simply by knowing what facts suicide bombers believe (perhaps that Allah rewards martyrs). But, of course, such a world is so foreign to our own that no matter how many facts we learn about it, we still have a hard time really making sense of it.

This is why Heidegger says specifically that 'any understanding (*Verständnis*) has its being in an act of understanding (*Verstehen*)'. For Heidegger, an understanding isn't something we possess (a collection of facts or bits of knowledge), but something we do. Dasein's understanding is found in the way that Dasein does things. My understanding of cooking, for example, is found in the way I handle food, kitchen implements, stoves and ovens, cookbooks. It is not found in my ability to produce true assertions about cooking, or my readiness to assent to true propositions about cooking. In just the same way, a true understanding of a world doesn't amount to knowing facts about it, but knowing how to live in it. Indeed, it might be the case that the more at home we are in our world, the fewer 'facts' we know about the world – what we understand becomes so obvious that we have a hard time noticing it, let alone articulating it. As Heidegger notes, 'familiarity with the world does not necessarily require that the relations which are constitutive for the world as the world should be theoretically transparent'. Rather, familiarity with the world is found in intuitively understanding why things are done the way that they are.

Living in a world, we all experience everyday actions, like driving to work, objects, like offices and desks, and people, like customers and supervisors, as coordinated with each other in a meaningful and orderly way. I demonstrate that I understand the world by performing actions in the right manner and for the appropriate purpose, by using objects correctly in the proper context, and by dealing with people appropriately. By contrast, if I didn't understand the world I find myself in, I would fail to act properly or to perform the appropriate action in a given circumstance; I wouldn't know what objects are, how to use them, and how they relate to other objects. I would consequently do inappropriate things with the objects and people around me.

'Appropriateness' here is dictated by what works or doesn't work in the world as it is organized. This is a function not only of the way things and activities are organized, but also of our well-settled expectations and dispositions to act that result from that organization. Appropriateness is not merely a result of the way that we might happen to *feel* about things. One can't appropriately use a sledgehammer to crack eggs for a soufflé. This is in part because of the physical properties of sledgehammers and eggs, but also in part because of the social practices and dispositions we have for soufflés – we eat them, and we don't like to have crunchy eggshells in them. We sometimes say that children, for example, are 'in their own world' because they lack the understanding of how things work, as well as the attitudes and dispositions that adults have about things. Growing up is, in large part, a process of being introduced into a sense of what is appropriate and inappropriate in the adult world – a sense that we, as adults, intuitively grasp.

Movies and novels love to explore the failures of understanding that result when, for example, aliens or time travellers find themselves in a strange world. They constantly find themselves in perplexing situations because they don't understand how to act or how to relate objects and actions to one another. A real-world case of an encounter with another world occurred in 1991 when a 5,000-year-old mummy was discovered in a melting Alpine glacier. The 'iceman' was extremely well preserved, and was found with a variety of sophisticated tools. Of the wooden tools, a researcher notes:

> the variety of tree species represented is astonishing. This is no accident. Every implement is subject to certain, often very disparate demands, so the chosen raw material must satisfy particular ergonomic and technological preconditions. For his

equipment the Iceman invariably chose the best-suited
materials. This calls for considerable experience of a kind
virtually lost to our own civilization. (Spindler, p. 216)

Understanding what exactly tools were and how they were
used sometimes requires 'experimental anthropology',
research that reconstructs the meaning of ancient objects by
building reproductions of them and then actually trying to use
them together with the other things that would have been
present in the ancient environment.

Like the experimental anthropologists, we all are introduced into a world as babies by being taught to do things.
Knowing *what* to do, we could say, is a necessary condition of
understanding a world. In Heidegger's way of putting it, the
involvements that things have with each other 'must be disclosed beforehand with a certain intelligibility'. We must see
things as being intelligibly put to such and such a use, for such
and such a purpose. That we see this 'beforehand' means that
we don't have to deliberately say to ourselves (as the experimental anthropologist undoubtedly does at some point) 'this
funny object with the blunt heavy thing at the end – this must
be used to pound things'. Instead, we simply see it straight off
as a hammer.

While seeing *what* to do with things is essential to understanding a world, we only really inhabit a world when we also
intuitively see that these are *the right things* to do, that it *makes sense*
to do them in this way. As Heidegger observes, in understanding
a world, Dasein does things 'in terms of a potentiality-for-being
for the sake of which it itself is'. Each world gives us different
potentialities-for-being, different ways that I can be or can live. In
the world of Texas politics, one could be a politician or a jour-
nalist, but there's no room for kings and dukes. When I inhabit
the world, I settle on one of these ways to be, and henceforth do

everything else for the sake of being that kind of person. Everything in the world now shows up in terms of this decision I have made about my existence.

Heidegger believes that the world structures activities by providing us with different possible ways to give order to our lives. These are potential ways to be, for the sake of which we do everything else. All the different activities we engage in are ordered in terms of (they 'ultimately go back to') these ways of being. Suppose that, as I am digging a hole in my garden, someone asks me: 'Why? To what end? What are you digging the hole for?' I answer: 'So I can plant that tree.' This person asks again: 'What for?' I reply: 'So I can have fresh peaches in the fall.' 'What for?' 'So I can bake peach pies.' 'What for?' 'So I can nurture my family.' 'What for?' 'So I can be a good father.' At this point, if my inquisitive companion asks again 'What for?', I can offer no further answer. I have reached that for the sake of which I do everything else. By providing us with certain possibilities for being (like being a Viking chieftain, a rock guitarist or a suicide bomber), a world ends up imposing an order and a meaning on activities. Conversely, in a world where, for example, being a suicide bomber is not a 'potentiality-for-being', all kinds of possible actions (strapping on an explosives-laden vest) will be excluded as making no sense.

In the same way, the world will end up actually giving structure to the objects that appear in the world. As Heidegger puts it, the world 'lets an entity be encountered', it 'sets it free' to play a role. One might think that when we 'let a spade be encountered' or 'set a spade free', these are deliberate actions on our part, actions by which we turn some physical object into a spade (perhaps by forging the blade from steel and turning the handle from wood). A spade is not merely a physical object with certain physical properties like colour, mass, density, shape, etc. It does have those physical properties, of course, but it only becomes a *spade* (as opposed to a *hard, heavy object*) when it can be aligned with activities like shovelling and other entities like gardens and trenches. Thus, the spade is set free to be a spade by the existence of a world, on the basis of which an ordered set of activities and practices are possible. We contribute to letting things be through our active understanding of the world, for in understanding the world, we let ourselves into a space where actions involving the spade are possible.

So how is it with the spade, then, when we take it up and use it? Imagine that one is confronting an array of tools – a round-nosed shovel, a pointed shovel, a trenching shovel, a snow shovel. How do we decide which one to use? They have this much in common: they are all *serviceable* for digging. What they are serviceable for groups them together as shovels and distinguishes them from other tools like picks, wheelbarrows and kitchen blenders. But they are distinguished from each other by what they are *useable* for. The snow shovel is not able to dig through compacted soil. The trenching shovel cannot move large quantities of loose material like snow. Suppose, then, that one selects the pointed shovel because one wishes to dig a hole in the garden for the purpose of planting a tree. In making this selection, one presupposes not just the customary uses of the shovel, but also the other entities with which the shovel will be employed. The dense soil dictates the selection of the pointed-nose shovel. In addition, the choice of a shovel takes into consideration not just the entity with which I use the shovel directly, but the entities alongside of which I will be digging. Such considerations would dictate other features of the shovel: if I were to dig the hole in very close quarters, I would select a short-handled shovel. Because I am digging a hole for the root ball of a tree, I will also use a tape measure to make sure the hole is not too deep. I will not, however, need to form a neat and clean hole the way I would if I were digging a trench for a sprinkler line, so I won't need the trenching shovel or round-nosed shovel.

Attention to these details might at first seem philosophically uninteresting, but they help us to see precisely how the world can affect the physical structure of things without the world itself being a physical entity. The actual make-up of the shovels is determined by the activities that we engage in which, as we saw above, is ultimately determined by the possible ways of being that the world makes available to us. If digging trenches didn't somehow help us pursue our ultimate goals – that for the sake of which we do everything else – it would be a meaningless activity in our world. As a result, there would be no trenching shovels. But the world reaches right down into the fine details of the structure of objects. It does this because, by opening up possibilities for being, and structuring activities, the world also determines the contexts in which things will be used. The shovel, depending on what role it plays in helping us realize our ends or goals, will be used *with* other particular objects – sandy or rocky soils, snow or wood chips. In Heidegger's terminology, it has a 'with-which'. Depending on the particular purpose served by the tool, and the particular things it is used on, it will have to be long or short, narrow or broad, pointed or rounded. Simply by giving us a sense for what is worth devoting our lives to, and what is not worthwhile, the world ends up having a profound impact on all the objects and activities with which we busy ourselves in our everyday lives.

But what exactly *is* the world? Heidegger tells us that the world is that in which we find ourselves. It is 'the

"wherein'" of an active understanding (i.e., an understanding manifested in our knowing what to do and why it makes
sense to do it). This kind of understanding is not located in
physical space the way that jam is located in a jar. If it were,
then the suicide bomber and the Texas politician would
inhabit the same world simply in virtue of inhabiting the
same space. Instead, the understanding *in*habits a domain of
possibilities. When I understand the world, I find myself in
a particular situation, where I have available to me different
'for-the-sake-of-whichs', different ways to give order and
purpose to my life. And when I settle on one of these
'potentialities-for-being', I will find that the world is set up
so as to permit particular activities and objects to be used in
pursuing this way of life.

The world, in conclusion, is that wherein all of our actions
make sense; and we understand it in knowing how to act. The
world has a structure articulated in terms of all the different
kinds of actions, purposes, roles and ways of organizing one's
life that are available to us within our culture. (Thus, we can
share the same world, even when we take up different roles,
because our actions intertwine and support each other.) As
Daseins, we are responsive to this world structure in all that
we do.

But a space of possibilities isn't itself the kind of entity
that the physical sciences can study directly. An anthropologist can work her way into this space by doing things, by
trying out the wooden tools of the iceman, for example,
but the space of possibilities will never be something that
can be measured or described objectively. It is something,
instead, that has to be understood to be seen. Heidegger
suggests that, to the extent that our reverence for the physical sciences makes us dismiss as unreal anything that can't
be scientifically theorized, we run the risk of overlooking

the world. That would, in turn, make it impossible to understand ourselves for, as we have seen, the world is that on the basis of which we act and in terms of which we relate to everything else around us.

3

THE STRUCTURE OF BEING-IN-THE-WORLD, PART 1: DISPOSEDNESS AND MOODS

[O]ntologically mood is a primordial kind of being for Dasein, in which Dasein is disclosed to itself *prior to* all cognition and volition, and *beyond* their range of disclosure . . . Ontologically, we thus obtain as the *first* essential characteristic of states-of-mind that *they disclose Dasein in its thrownness and – proximally and for the most part – in the manner of an evasive turning-away*.

. . . A mood assails us. It comes neither from 'outside' nor from 'inside', but arises out of being-in-the-world, as a way of such being. But with the negative distinction between state-of-mind and the reflective apprehending of something 'within', we have thus reached a positive insight into their character as disclosure. *The mood has already disclosed, in every case, being-in-the-world as a whole, and makes it possible first of all to direct oneself towards something.* Having a mood is not related to the psychical in the first instance, and is not itself an inner condition which then reaches forth in an enigmatical way and puts its mark on Things and persons. It is in this that the *second* essential characteristic of states-of-mind shows itself. We have seen that the world, Dasein-with, and existence are *equiprimordially disclosed*; and state-of-mind is a basic existential species of their disclosedness, because this disclosedness itself is essentially being-in-the-world.

Besides these two essential characteristics of states-of-mind which have been explained – the disclosing of thrownness and the current disclosing of being-in-the-world as a whole – we have to notice a *third*, which contributes above all towards a more penetrating understanding of the worldhood of the world . . . [T]o be affected by the unserviceable, resistant, or threatening character of that which is ready-to-hand, becomes ontologically possible only in so far as being-in as such has been determined existentially beforehand in such a manner that what it encounters within-the-world can '*matter*' *to* it in this way. The fact that this sort of thing can 'matter' to it is grounded in one's state-of-mind; and as a state-of-mind it has already disclosed the world – as something by which it can be threatened, for instance. Only something which is in the state-of-mind of fearing (or fearlessness) can discover that what is environmentally ready-to-hand is threatening. Dasein's openness to the world is constituted existentially by the attunement of a state-of-mind . . . Under the strongest pressure and resistance, nothing like an affect would come about . . . if being-in-the-world, with its state-of-mind, had not already submitted itself to having entities within-the-world 'matter' to it in a way which its moods have outlined in advance. *Existentially, a state-of-mind implies a disclosive submission to the world, out of which we can encounter something that matters to us.* (*Being and Time*, pp. 175–7)

Being and Time has enormous implications for the way we think about what it means to be human. By demonstrating that human beings are essentially defined by the way they exist in a world, and by spelling out what follows from this, Heidegger has shown how better to understand certain aspects of our own existence that might otherwise be puzzling. As long as we think, for example, that what is really important about human beings is their rationality – an assumption shared by philosophers from Plato to Kant and beyond – the passions present us with something of a paradox. On the one hand, a life devoid of passions like love, joy and hope holds little attraction to us. On the other hand, the passions seem profoundly irrational – they often make no sense, they can disrupt our ability to think clearly and rationally about a matter, and they frequently refuse to submit to our better judgement. The struggle between our reason and our emotions is one manifestation of a fundamental feature of our being – the way that we are never completely free to act, or completely determined by forces outside of our control.

For those who admire the ideal of a fully rational existence, it is a source of frustration that we can neither ever finally master our moods, nor completely control the world that shapes and encompasses us. For Heidegger, to the contrary, a lack of complete control is no failing or shortcoming, but the very condition that makes it possible to 'encounter something that matters to us'. The essence of human existence is always to find ourselves in between freedom from and submission to our world. As we have seen, Heidegger's preferred name for the kind of entities we are is 'Dasein', which means literally 'there-being'. To be a Dasein is to always exist in a 'there', a meaningful and particular setting for action. I am here in my office, in the twenty-first century, enchanted by the book I am reading, living out my existence as a college professor. This is my 'there', and every Dasein always finds itself in some such 'there'. My 'there' itself is shot through with the tension between my freedom to decide my own life, and my subjection to things I can't decide. Another related tension between our freedom within and subjection to the 'there' is manifest in our particular moods. Moods are, Heidegger believes, instances of a general structure of our being that he calls 'state-of-mind' – that is, our way of being disposed to the world. The phrase 'state-of-mind' is, however, a very bad translation of Heidegger's term *Befindlichkeit*, and I will use in its place the more accurate 'disposedness'.[4]

To understand what Heidegger says about moods and dis-posedness, let's first try to get a feel for the phenomena he is talking about. Think for a moment about what it is like to be in a mood, to feel fearful, for example. (Heidegger himself considers this example in *Being and Time*, pp. 180–82). Imagine that you are walking down an unfamiliar alley, enjoy-ing the tranquillity of a dark night, when suddenly you hear a rustling noise behind you, followed by urgent approaching footsteps. You feel certain bodily changes, although you are probably not distinctly aware of them: a quickening of the pulse, a tensing of your muscles. You pick up your pace, glance around for other people or for ways to escape the alley. You become focused on the end of the alley, and start to anticipate possible responses to a potential assailant. Every-thing looks different than it did a moment before, and you suddenly notice things to which you hadn't previously paid any attention (you see distinctly a side alley as a possible escape route, you strain to discern noises that you had been com-pletely unaware of a moment before). By the same token, things you had previously been attending to disappear. In a moment, the tranquillity of the night, your appreciation of the moonlight, your pleasant recollections of the evening have been swept away as you feel yourself threatened.

If we pay attention to experiences like this, we learn first of all, as Heidegger notes, that 'moods assail us'. Heidegger's German term for 'assail' is *überfallen*, a much more picturesque expression. It means literally 'to fall upon suddenly', and thus 'to surprise', 'to assault', 'to take or seize'. In other words, it is not wholly up to us how we will be affected by the situations we find ourselves in; there is a necessary element of passivity to them. If a friend tells me to cheer up, for example, I can't simply will myself to be cheerful. Instead, I need to do things and put myself into the kinds of situations where cheerfulness can come over me. So moods are not something subjective in the classical sense – they don't come 'from "inside"', and I don't subjectively project them over the situation: 'Having a mood is not related to the psychical in the first instance, and is not itself an inner condition which then reaches forth in an enigmatical way and puts its mark on things and persons.' The fear in the alleyway does not come from me, any more than cheerfulness does. We are right to say that the alley *really is* frightening, a room or party *really is* cheerful. That such moods are not merely subjective is also supported by the fact that there are public moods. We can share with others the fear or the good cheer or the hopefulness of a certain situation (say, the home side scoring a goal in the ninetieth minute of a tied match).

Moods are no more fully objective than they are merely subjective. They don't come to me 'from "outside"'. The dark alleyway isn't objectively fearsome; it is not the case that everyone would be afraid there, or even that I would always experience fear while walking through it. Moods, as Heidegger says in our passage, 'arise out of being-in-the-world'. Moods come from a whole way of comporting ourselves and relating ourselves to the things and people around us.

Let's summarize what we have learned through our consideration of the example of fear. First, the fear I feel in the alleyway shows me how I stand with respect to the world around me – it shows me how I am vulnerable in relation to what is threatening me, how I am needy in relation to what offers sanctuary, etc. Next, we saw that it makes the situation as a whole show up differently, and allows me to focus on and direct myself towards particular things within that whole. Finally, when I fear, I experience things as mattering to me in a particular way, as being important or irrelevant. All these characteristics together show my submission to the world – I take the world as it shows itself to me, find myself in reference to this world, and accept the world's determination of how I should act. I simply have to accept the fact that, because I don't have means to defend myself in the alleyway, and because of the aggressor's size, strength and weapons, it doesn't make sense to turn and confront my aggressor. But it does make sense to run.

'Disposedness' names the structure implicit in this description of fear. Fear is just one way of relating to the situation we find ourselves in. Happiness, anger, indifference, indeed all the other moods will relate us to our surroundings in different ways. Heidegger's account of disposedness is meant to show us what is common to all the different moods, all the different ways that we find ourselves 'in between' freedom to act and submission to the world. In particular, he identifies three essential characteristics of disposedness that correspond to the features of our experience of fear.

Here's what Heidegger tells us in the extract above: first, disposedness 'discloses Dasein in its thrownness'; second, that disposedness 'discloses being-in-the-world as a whole'; and finally, that disposedness is our 'submission to the world, out of which we can encounter something that matters to us' (or, as Heidegger says elsewhere, Dasein 'constantly surrenders itself to the 'world' and lets the 'world' 'matter' to it: *Being and Time*, p. 178).

'Thrownness' is Heidegger's name for the way that we always find ourselves 'thrown' into or 'delivered over' to circumstances that are beyond our control. We discovered that, in feeling fear, we could neither control how we felt nor how the situation was configured. In just the same way, from the moment of birth until our death, we are subject to things about which we have little if any say: who our parents are, where and when we live, what colour our skin or our eyes are, what kind of natural resources or other people are to be found in our environs. We also find ourselves submitted to a certain set of possible ways to live our lives – today we can be auto mechanics or journalists, but we can't be druids or pharaohs. Of course, we can within certain limits alter our 'thrownness', but we are even thrown into and must submit to the possible ways of altering the situation we are thrown into. It is a structural feature of human existence that we always find ourselves thrown into such circumstances, and that we exist in the ways made available by this thrownness.

With the second claim about disposedness, that it 'discloses being-in-the-world as a whole', Heidegger is pointing to the way that while we are in a mood, everything shows up as having a certain unified 'tone' or 'flavour' or 'feel'. When we are bored, everything shows up as either boring or important to the degree that it offers us a way to distract ourselves from the boredom we feel. We saw how fear makes the situation as a whole show up differently than it did when the mood was one of tranquillity – when we are frightened, things show up to the degree that they are threatening us or allowing us to escape from the threat. But, far from distorting the reality of the situation,[5] this polarizing effect 'makes it possible first of all to direct oneself towards something'. Moods do this by deciding for us what will be salient in the given situation, or what will withdraw into inconspicuousness. Without this, the world would offer a bewildering number of features and facets – too many to cope with effectively.

Finally, disposedness is a kind of submission to the world which allows things to matter to us. We saw how, in fear, the situation into which we are thrown dictates the possibilities available to us. Through our fear, certain possibilities become important, others unimportant. The way things matter to us, Heidegger sees, is not something that we are free to decide, but is imposed on us by the way the world is arranged and the ways that we are disposed for the world. Letting things be encountered in a particular way, Heidegger notes in our passage, is 'primarily circumspective; it is not just sensing something or staring at it'. 'Circumspection' should be heard in the literal sense of 'looking around'. It is, for Heidegger, the kind of seeing or experiencing of the world that we have when our relation to things takes its measure from the other things and projects with which we are involved. As I lay marble tiles in my sitting room, for example, I see the tiles with other things 'in view' – the mortar and other tiles and fireplace and the finished project. I see each particular thing by seeing it with regard to the other things around it and possible projects in which to use it. This kind of seeing, then, takes in and responds to the situation as it unfolds in light of my projects. And this kind of seeing, as Heidegger notes in our passage, always has a mood – a way of having submitted ourselves to and been affected by the world.

Being-in-the-world, to summarize, involves our always finding ourselves in the world in a particular way. We have a 'there', that is, a meaningfully structured situation in which to act and exist. One constitutive element of there-being is that the world is always disposed or arranged in a particular way that we cannot fully control. Another element is that we ourselves are always disposed to things in a particular way; they always matter to us somehow or other. The way things matter is manifest in our moods, which govern and structure our comportment by disposing us in different ways to things in the world. So disposedness is an 'attunement', a way of being tuned in to things in the world, and tuned by the things of the world. This disposedness is something we can never fully master. But far from that being a detriment to our freedom, it is the condition that first makes it possible. It makes things matter to us, and makes us ready to deal with the things we encounter. Without that, we'd have no basis for action at all.

4

THE STRUCTURE OF BEING-IN-THE-WORLD, PART 2: UNDERSTANDING AND INTERPRETATION

As understanding, Dasein projects its being upon possibilities. This *being-towards-possibilities* which understands is itself a potentiality-for-being, and it is so because of the way these possibilities, as disclosed, exert their counter-thrust upon Dasein. The projecting of the understanding has its own possibility – that of developing itself. This development of the understanding we call 'interpretation'. In it the understanding appropriates understandingly that which is understood by it. In interpretation, understanding does not become something different. It becomes itself. Such interpretation is grounded existentially in understanding; the latter does not arise from the former. Nor is interpretation the acquiring of information about what is understood; it is rather the working-out of possibilities projected in understanding . . .

In terms of the significance which is disclosed in understanding the world, concernful being-alongside the ready-to-hand gives itself to understand whatever involvement that which is encountered can have. To say that 'circumspection discovers' means that the 'world' which has already been understood comes to be interpreted. The ready-to-hand comes *explicitly* into the sight which understands. All preparing, putting to rights, repairing, improving, rounding-out, are accomplished in the following way: we take apart in its 'in-order-to' that which is circumspectively ready-to-hand, and we concern ourselves with it in accordance with what becomes visible through this process. That which has been circumspectively taken apart with regard to its 'in-order-to', and taken apart as such – that which is *explicitly* understood – has the structure of *something as something*. The circumspective question as to what this partic- ular thing that is ready-to-hand may be, receives the circumspectively interpretative answer that it is for such and such a purpose. If we tell what it is for, we are not simply desig- nating something; but that which is designated is understood *as* that *as* which we are to take the thing in question. That which is disclosed in understanding – that which is understood – is already accessible in such a way that its 'as which' can be made to stand out explicitly. The 'as' makes up the structure of the explicitness of something that is understood. It constitutes the interpretation. In dealing with what is environmentally ready-to- hand by interpreting it circumspectively, we 'see' it *as* a table, a door, a carriage, or a bridge; but what we have thus interpreted need not necessarily be also taken apart by making an assertion which definitely characterizes it. Any mere pre-predicative seeing of the ready-to-hand is, in itself, something which already under- stands and interprets . . . When we have to do with anything, the mere seeing of the things which are closest to us bears in itself the structure of interpretation, and in so primordial a manner that just to grasp something *free*, as it were, *of the 'as'* requires a certain readjustment. When we merely stare at something, our just-having-it-before-us lies before us *as a failure to understand it any more*. This grasping which is free of the 'as' is a privation of the kind of seeing in which one *merely* understands. It is not more primordial than that kind of seeing, but is derived from it. If the 'as' is ontically unexpressed, this must not seduce us into overlooking it as a constitutive state for understanding, existen- tial and *a priori*. (*Being and Time*, pp. 188–90)

What could be more obvious than that we understand our world? Of course, there are always things we don't understand. But as I go about my everyday affairs, I more or less understand what I'm doing, the things I'm dealing with, the events that transpire around me. I see a painting, for example, Paul Klee's *The Goldfish*, and I understand immediately that I am looking at a painting of fish swimming in deep waters, that the fish in the centre is a goldfish, that the painting is a very valuable object, and an indefinite number of other facts about it.

And yet, if we accept the modernist view that science tells us what entities *really* are, our understanding of the world is just as mysterious as it is obvious. The simple act of seeing a painting, of understanding what it is to be a painting, seems to conceal an incomprehensibly complex process. After all, science tells us that we don't really see a *painting*; instead we see *light waves* reflected from the surface of a physical object. The reflective properties of the light waves are dictated by the physical structure of the paints, the canvass, the ambient lighting conditions, and so on. The light waves stimulate millions of photoreceptors in the retina. Somehow, science tells us, my brain processes the signals from my eyes, and converts them into an experience of a Klee masterpiece. But we don't literally see a masterpiece – we know this because light waves can't carry information about the institutions of Western art that make a painting a masterpiece. At most, they carry information about things like colours and shapes. That means that our understanding of the things we see is the complex product of a process carried out by our minds or brains on the pattern of stimulation provided by the physical events in the world. We *understand* when we take some brute physical fact *as* something, say, a painting of a goldfish.

So goes the conventional wisdom. Indeed, if anything has changed in the eighty years since Heidegger wrote *Being and Time*, it is that philosophers are increasingly willing to concede to science the task of explaining how our sensory inputs are processed into an understanding of the world.

Where the question is how the brain physically functions, philosophers naturally should yield to science. But does this mean that there is no longer any task for philosophy to play in explaining our understanding of the world? Only if our understanding of the world is contained in the brain. According to Heidegger, however, it is not the brain that understands, but the whole being in the world. And what we understand is not a brain state, but things in the world. Thus, Heidegger grants that all our experiences of things in the world involve an understanding and a kind of interpretation. We understand the painting, after all, *as* a painting. But understanding and interpretation are not brain states, they are ways of acting in the world.

Philosophy thus still has a task to perform, a task that can't be dispensed with by brain sciences. Philosophy can clarify the nature of the understanding and, in the process, help the sciences to know what it is that they should be trying to explain. For example, the idea that we discussed above – that our understanding is the result of processing brute physical facts about the world – misleads many into thinking that we first experience things as meaningless, and then proceed to impose a subjective meaning on them. But this is belied by our experience of the world. If we stay with the phenomena, we'll recognize that we see, for example, the painting right off *as* a painting. We don't, under normal circumstances, ever first see it as a meaningless concatenation of coloured patches, textures, and shapes, and then interpret it deliberately as a painting. Indeed, it takes 'a certain readjustment', a deliberate effort to look at things as strange in order to not see the object as something we understand. Our experience of the world is pervaded by an understanding of what things are, or how they are used. Even when we encounter something unfamiliar, we do it against the background of our basic understanding of the world. The unfamiliar shows up as out of place, implying that we see it only because we already understand what belongs here.

Our fundamental familiarity with and understanding of the world is the basis for everything that we do. I am free to act and to decide my own course in life only because I understand what it is possible for me to do. Without any understanding, the world would present us with a meaningless and confusing chaos. But at the same time that they liberate me, the possibilities that are open to me constrain me – they 'exert their counter-thrust upon' me. Like our moods and passionate ways of being disposed for the world, then, our fundamental understanding of the world frees us but also limits what we can do. A full appreciation of the human condition, and of our potential to decide on our own course of life, requires grasping how our understanding of the world works. It will require, in particular, seeing to what extent the way we currently understand things constrains what we can do, and likewise to what extent we can explore new possibilities for understanding the world.

What does it mean to say that I understand something? Heidegger describes understanding as a 'projecting upon possibilities'. He means that we understand something when we grasp the possible ways that it can be used, or the possible things that can happen to it. When I understand a pair of scissors, for example, then I understand it in terms of how it could relate to the other things in the world. Scissors are capable of cutting paper, cloth and string well. They could cut a cardboard box with some difficulty, and they could not cut an oak plank at all. Of course, we can understand scissors without having to catalogue all the things they can and can't cut, but we nevertheless don't understand them without some kind of intuitive sense for what they can and can't be used with. If my 'knowledge' of the scissors consisted simply in the recognition that they consist of two black–coloured ovals attached to long, triangular, shiny metallic things, no one would be tempted to say that I *understand* the scissors. To see something as a pair of scissors, then, is to grasp the kinds of possibilities for cutting things that they afford me. It follows that I don't have to be thinking about the scissors in order to understand them. Understanding is not, for Heidegger, an essentially cognitive act. I understand the scissors best when I have the bodily skills for using them – when my hands know how to grip them and manipulate them. Whether I think anything or believe any particular thing about them is irrelevant to deciding whether I understand them.

Notice, by the way, that the ways we habitually do things constrain the possibilities in terms of which we typically understand things. In one memorable scene from *Mr Bean*, for example, the title character uses his paper scissors to cut a bread roll to make a sandwich (he also dries his freshly washed lettuce by whirling it around inside his sock, and crushes his peppercorns with his shoe). It is possible to cut dinner rolls with scissors, but this is not a possibility in terms of which we typically understand the scissors. This fact points to the way that the world we inhabit constrains the range of what is possible. It is not the case that anything goes. This gives us more reason to doubt the conventional wisdom about brain processes constructing the world out of brute physical stimulations. According to the conventional wisdom, a painting isn't *really* a painting. We just take the stimulations produced by light waves streaming from the pigments on canvas *as* a painting. But Heidegger's description of the understanding helps us recognize that the structure of meaning that makes the painting a painting is built into the world; it is not a mere creation of my brain. Paintings belong to whole contexts of equipment and activities – they hang in galleries or over altars, they are bought and sold in auctions and stolen in daring heists, they have books written about them and, in some cases, laws exist for their protection. These worldly contexts are very real, and they structure the way we can relate to, use, and even look at paintings independently of whatever we happen to think about them. Information specifying an object as a masterpiece doesn't seem to be carried on light waves. And yet, that information is present in the world and available to be perceived if we have the skills that give us access to it.

My understanding of the world, then, consists in a grasp of the possible ways that the various objects and people around me relate to me and each other. This includes, most importantly, my own possibilities. There are lots of possible ways for me to be a human being. It is possible for me to be a musician or an attorney or a fisherman. Lots of possibilities are closed off, too, by my world – it is getting very difficult to be a tinker, and impossible to be a knight errant. Once I settle on a way to give my existence purpose, say, as a musician, the meaning of this choice is also understood when I grasp the different possible ways to pursue it. I could play the classical guitar or jazz guitar, I could perform other composers' music or my own. But I can't do just anything in the name of being a musician; I am constrained by the possible ways of musical being available in my world. In being a musician, in other words, I *project* or *press into* the possibilities opened up by my world. I understand my world, then, when I know how to do things in my world, which means, as Heidegger puts it, I know how to project into the possibilities opened up by my world.

We put our understanding to work by using it to do things. As we act on our understanding, we inevitably develop and refine what we, at first, only vaguely grasped and, in the process, we may develop new ways of understanding things. Heidegger calls such a process of taking up an understanding and making it our own 'interpretation'. Interpretation, as Heidegger notes in our passage, is 'the working-out of possibilities projected in the understanding'. Elsewhere, he describes interpretation as 'the mode of putting-into-effect of the understanding . . . specifically as the cultivation, appropriation, and preservation of what is discovered in the understanding' (*History of the Concept of Time,* p. 265, translation modified). In the excerpt above, Heidegger notes that in interpretation, the 'understanding appropriates [i.e., makes its own] understandingly that which is understood by it'. 'Interpretation' is to be read in the way we use it when we say that a musician interpreted Beethoven's late string quartets, or an actor interpreted Shakespeare's King Richard III. The actor or musician interprets by playing it in his or her own way and he or she can do this without either explicitly reflecting on the fact that he or she is offering an interpretation of it, or explicitly noting any particular feature of his or her interpretation. At the same time, the musician is not free to play any notes she wishes, the actor in *King Richard III* can't improvise his lines. They need to interpret the works within the range of possibilities opened up by those works themselves. Heidegger is emphatic that the interpretation is not necessarily 'an acquiring of information' (*Kenntnisnahme* – a better translation would be 'taking cognizance of') about what is understood. Instead, it is a taking-over and developing of possibilities. Thus, I don't have to think anything to myself while interpreting something. As Heidegger explains elsewhere, 'interpretation is carried out primordially not in a theoretical statement but in an action of circumspective concern – laying aside the unsuitable tool, or exchanging it, "without wasting words"' (*Being and Time,* p. 200). Interpretation, like understanding, is not essentially a cognitive act. We can explicitly and thematically interpret something as something by thinking deliberately about it or speaking and writing about it. But we can equally interpret it simply by using it.

Unlike most philosophers since Descartes, then, Heidegger has interpreted the essential human activities of seeing, understanding and interpreting as practical orientations to the world rather than mental states. When we see something, we always see it *as* something. But that doesn't mean we have to take a brute, meaningless entity and impose a subjective meaning on it. Rather, it means that we are always responding to the meanings built into the world itself. Seeing is, for Heidegger, intuitively grasping the possibilities for actively relating ourselves to a thing. Our understanding and interpretation of the world, as a consequence, are to be found in our living in those possibilities.

The philosophical emphasis on the mental aspects of human existence made it that much easier to concede to science the task of explaining human understanding. This is because mental states are obviously dependent in a straightforward way on brain states, so it's hard to resist thinking that we might be able to discover the physiological underpinnings of the mind. For philosophers influenced by Heidegger's emphasis on being-in-the-world, however, it is obvious that our understanding of the world is not reducible to a brain state. While Heidegger's view remains the minority view amongst philosophers and psychologists, his basic insight has been taken up and developed in important ways by subsequent thinkers. These include Merleau-Ponty's critique of mainstream psychological theories, Hubert Dreyfus's critique of mainstream cognitive sciences and certain research programmes in artificial intelligence, and Charles Taylor's critique of reductivist programmes in the social sciences.

5

EVERYDAYNESS AND THE 'ONE'

Dasein, as everyday being-with-one-another, stands in *subjection* to others. It itself *is* not; its being has been taken away by the others. Dasein's everyday possibilities of being are for the others to dispose of as they please. These others, moreover, are not *definite* others. On the contrary, any other can represent them. What is decisive is just that inconspicuous domination by others which has already been taken over unawares from Dasein as being-with. One belongs to the others oneself and enhances their power. 'The others' whom one thus designates in order to cover up the fact of one's belonging to them essentially oneself, are those who proximally and for the most part '*are there*' in everyday being-with-one-another. The 'who' is not this one, not that one, not oneself, not some people, and not the sum of them all. The 'who' is the neuter, the 'they'.

We have shown earlier how in the environment which lies closest to us, the public 'environment' already is ready-to-hand and is also a matter of concern. In utilizing public means of transport and in making use of information services such as the newspaper, every other is like the next. This being-with-one-another dissolves one's own Dasein completely into the kind of being of 'the others', in such a way, indeed, that the others, as distinguishable and explicit, vanish more and more. In this inconspicuousness and unascertainability, the real

dictatorship of the 'they' is unfolded. We take pleasure and
enjoy ourselves as *they* take pleasure; we read, see, and judge
about literature and art as *they* see and judge; likewise we
shrink back from the 'great mass' as *they* shrink back; we
find 'shocking' what *they* find shocking. The 'they', which is
nothing definite, and which all are, though not as the sum,
prescribes the kind of being of everydayness.

The 'they' has its own ways in which to be. That tendency of
being with which we have called 'distantiality' is grounded in
the fact that being-with-one-another concerns itself as such
with *averageness*, which is an existential characteristic of the
'they'. The 'they', in its being, essentially makes an issue of
this. Thus the 'they' maintains itself factically in the averageness of that which belongs to it, of that which it regards as
valid and that which it does not, and of that to which it grants
success and that to which it denies it. In this averageness with
which it prescribes what can and may be ventured, it keeps
watch over everything exceptional that thrusts itself to the fore.
Every kind of priority gets noiselessly suppressed. Overnight,
everything that is primordial gets glossed over as something
that has long been well known. Everything gained by a struggle
becomes just something to be manipulated. Every secret loses
its force. This care of averageness reveals in turn an essential
tendency of Dasein which we call the 'levelling down' of all
possibilities of being. (*Being and Time*, pp. 164–5)

With Descartes, Heidegger believed, modern philosophy took
a fateful wrong turn. It was fateful in the sense that it has
shaped the agenda for nearly every subsequent thinker. In his
effort to resist the Cartesian tradition in philosophy, Heidegger
returned often to the ancients – especially Aristotle and the
pre-Socratics – in an effort to discover a way out of what he
considered to be a philosophical dead end.

The crucial move that Descartes made was to suppose that
what we know are not the things in the world, but our ideas
of things. Descartes is most famous in the popular imagination

for his conclusion: 'I think, therefore I am.' He arrived at this conclusion by refusing to accept any belief of which he could not be absolutely certain. Even if he could be deceived about the existence of everything else, he reasoned, he could not be deceived about the fact that he was thinking because, in order to believe a false thought, one must be thinking – that is, entertaining beliefs. Descartes built his philosophical edifice on the indubitably certain belief that he could not be deceived about what he thought. This move was meant to place our understanding on solid ground, making it immune to doubt, because even if we lack certainty that what we think is true, we can't doubt our access to our own thoughts. But this achievement came at a terrible price. It threw into question our knowledge of the things outside our minds.

Descartes thus took as his paradigm case our false beliefs. When we believe something that is false, we are thinking a thought without thinking *about* anything that actually exists in the world. If one generalizes from the case of false beliefs, then it is easy to suppose that all one is really ever immediately acquainted with is one's thoughts. These thoughts may or may not represent the way that things are. In this regard, Descartes was faithfully followed by philosophers like Locke, Berkeley and Hume, all of whom supposed that we are, as it were, cut off from the world by a veil of ideas. Even Kant in his own way remained with the tradition, accepting that we do not have access to the things in themselves.

Once one supposes that all we know immediately or directly are our own thoughts or representations of things, it naturally becomes questionable whether we can really know that other people exist. After all, I have no direct access to the minds of other people. I am thus left to infer the existence of other minds. As Oxford philosopher A. J. Ayer explained it, 'the only ground that I can have for believing that other people have experiences, and that some at least of their experiences are of the same character as my own, is that their overt behaviour is similar to mine' (Ayer, pp. 346–7). But since we never have direct evidence that others are having experiences, it follows that the existence of others is never certain.

While modern philosophers brood over their inability to prove the obvious – for example, that we are not alone in the world – modern social critics worry about the undeniable impact of others on our personal lives. As technology improves the efficiency of educational, economic and governmental mechanisms for the control of life, these critics have grown increasingly anxious that we are not isolated enough from the effects of other people. Modern society is an increasingly normalized society, where fewer and fewer idiosyncrasies are tolerated or indulged in. Oscar Wilde, for example, complained that:

> few people ever 'possess their souls' before they die. 'Nothing is more rare in any man,' says Emerson, 'than an act of his own.' It is quite true. Most people are other people. Their thoughts are some one else's opinions, their lives a mimicry, their passions a quotation. (Wilde, p. 105)

As if to emphasize the rarity of an original thought, Wilde quotes someone else to show that even his critique of conformity is unoriginal. Like Wilde, Emerson and other thinkers such as Nietzsche and Kierkegaard, Heidegger is concerned about the dangers of conformism in modern society. But he also saw that this tendency towards normalized forms of behaviour is not something we could or should want to overcome completely. It is, instead, an essential part of what it is to be human. And, in a brilliant stroke, Heidegger saw that our essential 'being-with-others' holds the key to disarming the modern philosopher's solipsistic worries that we can never know the existence of other minds.

If we pay attention to our ordinary, everyday experiences of the world, it is obvious that other Daseins are already built into our understanding of and dispositions for the world. The meanings of the ordinary, everyday things with which we are most familiar are intrinsically shaped by the fact that they belong to a world we share in common with other beings like ourselves. In a lecture course he taught in 1925 while writing *Being and Time*, Heidegger offered the following kinds of examples:

> The tool I am using is bought by someone, the book is a gift from . . . the umbrella is forgotten by someone. The dining-table at home is not a round top on a stand but a piece of furniture in a particular place, which itself has its particular places at which particular others are seated everyday. (*History of the Concept of Time*, p. 239)

In addition, as we go about our everyday affairs, we encounter other people as Daseins, with their own ways of understanding and interpreting things, their own possibilities, identities and moods. Indeed, many of our activities are activities for others, or activities in which we must deal with others. 'Being-with,' Heidegger notes, 'is an existential constituent of being-in-the-world . . . So far as Dasein *is* at all, it has being-with-one-another as its kind of being' (*Being and Time*, p. 163).

In the excerpt that opens this chapter, Heidegger focuses on being-with in one particular mode – the 'everyday being-with-one-another', or being-with in the mode of *das Man*, 'the they' or 'the one'. *Man* is an indefinite pronoun in German, and it is used in expressions like 'they say that . . .' (*man sagt dass . . .*), 'one must do it' (*man muss es tun*), or 'that's just what one does' (*man macht das eben so*). In what follows, I will usually use the term 'the one' rather than 'the they'. When we say in English 'that's just what one does', it implies both that one *should* do it that way, and that there is no one in particular who has decided that one should do it that way. When we say 'that's just what they do', we lose both those implications. Heidegger's claim here is that, in the first instance and most of the time, we relate to others in the mode of 'the one', which means that we understand ourselves in terms of what one says about the way one should live, that is, in terms of what one ordinarily does in situations that confront us.

At stake, then, is the role that social relations play in making us who we are. Before we ever really begin thinking or making decisions for ourselves, the people with whom we live have introduced us to a particular understanding of ourselves and the world around us. This means that I am never in a position to decide for myself how I will understand things from the ground up, or to invent my own way of being in the world independently of any relationship to other human beings. Every innovation, every act of rebellion, every independent decision is shaped by our shared understandings and norms of behaviour. Rebellion, for instance, is always rebellion against something, and gets its character as a rebellious act from the very thing it rejects.

The meaning of nearly everything we encounter or everything we do, then, is informed to a considerable degree by the fact that we always inhabit a shared world with others, and the way we exist in this world is always essentially structured by others: 'The world of Dasein is a with-world' (*Being and Time*, p. 155). As a result, our understanding and interpretation of the world is always, at least initially, the understanding and interpretation dictated by the way that others understand and interpret things. Of course, we can, within limits, arrive at our own authentic understanding of the world. But, as Heidegger notes,

> there is not a little which never gets beyond . . . an average understanding. This everyday way in which things have been interpreted is one into which Dasein has grown in the first instance, with never a possibility of extrication. In it, out of it, and against it, all genuine understanding, interpreting, and communicating, all re-discovering and appropriating anew, are performed. In no case is a Dasein, untouched and unseduced by this way in which things have been interpreted, set before the open country of a 'world-in-itself', so that it just beholds what it encounters. (*Being and Time*, p. 213)

The same goes for our moods and ways of being disposed for the world:

> The dominance of the public way in which things have been interpreted has already been decisive even for the possibilities of having a mood – that is, for the basic way in which Dasein lets the world 'matter' to it. The 'one' prescribes one's state-of-mind [disposedness], and determines what and how one 'sees'. (*Being and Time*, p. 213)

Because others play a decisive role in making me who I am, there is no genuine 'other minds' problem. We don't have to infer that others exist, because we are constantly in contact with them. The real question is not 'are there others?', but rather 'can I be myself?' For it turns out that, at least in the everyday existence which immediately structures my world, my essence is not dictated by me, but by others.

Our most fundamental experience of other Daseins – our experience of 'those who proximally and for the most part "are there" in everyday being-with-one-another' – is,

Heidegger explains, of having our basic possibilities for being dictated to us by social norms: 'Dasein, as everyday being-with-one-another, stands in subjection to others. It itself is not: its being has been taken away by the others. Dasein's everyday possibilities of being are for the others to dispose of as they please.' What hobbies we pursue in our spare time, the TV shows we watch, the kind of things we talk about, the kinds of food we eat, the ways we dress, the vocations we pursue, our opinions on current events – all this is determined by others, because they provide us with the equipment we can use and the opportunities we can pursue as we go about our everyday affairs.

Who are these others who decide what I can do and how I can do it? Heidegger points out that there is no definite answer to this question. Even if we can identify a particular individual or group of individuals who started a trend or set a style, that individual or group could not make the trend or style become trendy or stylish, nor can they make us feel compelled to go along with the trend. Matt Groening, for instance, may be the creator of *The Simpsons*, but he didn't and couldn't make it hip to watch *The Simpsons*. Instead, it's hip because everyone says it is. We might be able to trace the genesis of particular practices and entities, in other words, but ultimately no definite person or group of people is responsible for those practices becoming dominant cultural practices, and those entities becoming central to our way of being-in-the-world.

If there's no one in particular who decides such things, how is it that we are dominated by a common understanding of things? Part of the answer, Heidegger suggests, can be found in the way that our shared public world is structured. Activities and entities are aligned with one another so as to foster some dispositions and practices on our part and discourage others. As we learn to use the things that surround us in our shared world, we are subtly introduced into habits and practices and dispositions that we share with others because they, too, have learned by using the same things. Take Heidegger's example of public transportation: riding the Paris Métro requires a quite specific set of bodily skills and dispositions. We need to learn how to read a Métro map and where to look to discover the signs that tell us which Métro station we are in, or where to find the train we need. We must learn to use a Métro ticket. We need to learn where to stand to board the trains, how to open the doors, and how to stand or sit in the train. In doing all this, the physical structure of the Métro and the practices of the other Métro-riders guide us into certain practices – practices we come to share with all the other riders. Once we have become skilled Métro-riders ourselves, we join the others in enforcing and normalizing the practices. Heidegger extends this analysis to the dispositions and practices which govern our taste for the world – our publicly shared environment includes practices for dress and fashion, practices for conversation and expression, and so on. As we pick up the newspaper, turn on the TV, and banter with neighbours in the front yard, we are introduced to the ways in which one thinks and talks about all the matters of the day. Heidegger calls the result the 'dictatorship of the "one"': 'We take pleasure and enjoy ourselves as one takes pleasure; we read, see, and judge about literature and art as one sees and judges; likewise we shrink back from the "great mass" as one shrinks back; we find "shocking" what one finds shocking. The "one", which is nothing definite, and which all are, though not as the sum, prescribes the kind of being of everydayness.' We end up sharing with others a sense for the range of opinions and activities that are permissible, and even what constitutes success in life.

The tone of Heidegger's remarks about the 'one', for example his describing it as a 'dictatorship', might lead one to think that he rejects all conformity. But that's not true – Heidegger does recognize that having settled, normalized practices and expectations is not necessarily a bad thing. It would be a disaster if you constantly had to decide on every little thing that you were going to do (what to wear, what to eat, which side of the road to drive on, etc.). By organizing our common world, conformity provides the basis upon which we are free to make important decisions. Nevertheless, Heidegger agrees with Wilde's sentiments that the surrender to conformity leads to consequences we might not wish to accept – namely, a conformism in which it is all too easy never to take a stand for oneself.

Even when we resist the public norms of success and validity, we constantly take measure of the way we differ from the normal, average, ordinary ways of being. Heidegger calls our constant concern about how we differ from others or measure up to them 'distantiality'. Our distantiality tends to level down our practices, understandings and expectations to the 'average' – that is, to something comprehensible and acceptable to the great mass of our fellows. The norms that govern things are the norms available to anyone – thus the banality of the public world as everything unusual gets dumbed down or normalized into a form that makes it publicly acceptable.

'Distantiality' also tends towards 'disburdening' (*Being and Time*, p. 165) – that is, a willingness to accept the judgement of the others, thereby freeing ourselves from the need to take responsibility for the decisions we make. The result is that no one in particular ever really decides how things should be done – for example, how one is supposed to dress for a day at the office – but there is nevertheless a way that one does it. If you 'have any tendency to take things easily and make them easy', this disburdens you of the need to decide for yourself. Once again, this need not be a bad thing in itself as one ought not to burden oneself with every decision. But the danger is that I will so thoroughly disburden myself that I am, in the end, not myself at all, I am the 'one'. Heidegger calls this sort of conformism 'inauthenticity'. But authentic being – a being in which I take responsibility for myself – is only a 'modification of the "one"' which, after all, establishes the meaningfulness of the world within which I can be authentic. This leaves open the question exactly *how* to be *my own* self in inhabiting the world.

6

DEATH AND AUTHENTICITY

The closest closeness which one may have in being towards death as a possibility, is as far as possible from anything actual. The more unveiledly this possibility gets understood, the more purely does the understanding penetrate into it *as the possibility of the impossibility of any existence at all.* Death, as possibility, gives Dasein nothing to be 'actualized', nothing which Dasein, as actual, could itself *be.* It is the possibility of the impossibility of every way of comporting oneself towards anything, of every way of existing . . .

Death is Dasein's *ownmost* possibility. Being towards this possibility discloses to Dasein its *ownmost* potentiality-for-being, in which its very being is the issue. Here it can become manifest to Dasein that in this distinctive possibility of its own self, it has been wrenched away from the 'they'. This means that in anticipation any Dasein can have wrenched itself away from the 'they' already. But when one understands that this is something which Dasein 'can' have done, this only reveals its factical lostness in the everydayness of the they-self.

The ownmost possibility is *non-relational.* Anticipation allows Dasein to understand that that potentiality-for-being in which its ownmost being is an issue, must be taken over by Dasein alone. Death does not just 'belong' to one's own Dasein in an undifferentiated way; death *lays claim* to it as an *individual* Dasein. The non-relational character of death, as understood in anticipation, individualizes Dasein down to itself. This individualizing is a way in which the 'there' is disclosed for existence. It makes manifest that all being-alongside the things with which we concern ourselves, and all being-with others, will fail us when our ownmost potentiality-for-being is the issue. Dasein can be *authentically itself* only if it makes this possible for itself of its own accord. But if concern and solicitude fail us, this does not signify at all that these ways of Dasein have been cut off from its authentically being-its-self. As structures essential to Dasein's constitution, these have a share in conditioning the possibility of any existence whatsoever. Dasein is authentically itself only to the extent that, *as* concernful being-alongside and solicitous being-with, it projects itself upon its ownmost potentiality-for-being rather than upon the possibility of the they-self. The entity which anticipates its non-relational possibility, is thus forced by that very anticipation into the possibility of taking over from itself its ownmost being, and doing so of its own accord.

The ownmost, non-relational possibility is *not to be outstripped*. Being towards this possibility enables Dasein to understand that giving itself up impends for it as the uttermost possibility of its existence. Anticipation, however, unlike inauthentic being-towards-death, does not evade the fact that death is not to be outstripped; instead, anticipation frees itself *for* accepting this. When, by anticipation, one becomes free *for* one's own death, one is liberated from one's lostness in those possibilities which may accidentally thrust themselves upon one; and one is liberated in such a way that for the first time one can authentically understand and choose among the factical possibilities lying ahead of that possibility which is not to be outstripped. Anticipation discloses to existence that its uttermost possibility lies in giving itself up, and thus it shatters all one's tenaciousness to whatever existence one has reached. (*Being and Time*, pp. 306–8)

Heidegger's philosophy stands squarely in the existential tradition in Western thought, a tradition which holds that all philosophy must be grounded in our personal, engaged involvement in the world. Existentialists emphasize passion over rational detachment, human freedom over the mechanistic workings of the physical universe, and the groundlessness and arbitrariness of our way of life, as opposed to trusting in the ultimate rationality of the world. Like Pascal, Kierkegaard, Dostoevsky and Nietzsche before him, and like the French existentialists inspired by him, Heidegger thought that we have no option but to begin philosophical inquiry from a reflection on our current situation – our existence. In this, he is the faithful follower of Kierkegaard (1813–1855), who reminded us that 'philosophizing is not speaking fantastically to fantastical beings but speaking to existing individuals' (p. 121). Beginning with Plato, philosophers had sought to discover timeless 'forms', the unchanging and pure ideas that lie behind all the particular, changing, corruptible objects we perceive in the world. The existentialist thinker, by contrast, denies that we have any direct access to timeless metaphysical truths. All our understanding is mediated by the historical and social categories that shape the world we find ourselves in. That means that we have to figure out for ourselves how to live, what kind of norms we should follow. This is disconcerting, as we seem to need to believe that our lives have a profound meaning and purpose, that they are not just an accident of where we happen to have been born.

Like other existentialists, Heidegger believed that the normal response to the contingency of existence is to 'flee' from it – to try to ignore or deceive ourselves about the fact that our way of life is neither necessary nor the 'right' or 'true' way to be a human. One tries to throw oneself wholeheartedly and unthinkingly into our cultural norms but, the existentialists assert, we nevertheless realize, at least dimly, that we don't have to live the way that we do. Existentialist thinkers claim that we may well discover, in moments of despair, that we can no longer conceal our underlying anxiety over the seeming meaninglessness, banality and emptiness of devoting one's life to merely doing what one does in one's culture.

Heidegger believed that there is no way to relieve ourselves of this anxiety, because there is no such thing as a final, definitive, true ideal of how to live a life. But he also thought that, in surrendering our understanding and our choices to what 'they' say or what 'one' does, we renounce what is most essential about ourselves as human beings: the ability to take responsibility for choosing our own way to be, that is, the ability to be authentic.

Being authentic is no simple task. It takes a great effort at 'clearing-away concealments and obscurities', Heidegger writes, if I am to 'discover the world in my own way' (*Being and Time*, p. 167). I can discover the world in my own way because, unlike other entities like plants and animals, Dasein's way of being in the world isn't fixed or necessitated by forces outside of its control. The source of our anxiety – the fact that our ways of organizing the world are contingent, and ultimately not grounded in anything timeless and essential – is also the source of our greatest dignity as beings. We can change how we use and relate to the things around us. In the process, we can change the significance those things hold. The way we understand ourselves is always open to question, our being is always an issue yet to be resolved. To flee from our anxiety over the world – to try to deceive ourselves about the contingency of our lives by affirming our social norms as if they somehow reveal the final, ultimate truth about how one should live – is to fail to realize what is unique about us – our ability to be authentic, to discover the world in our own way. Death, though, offers us an opportunity to take responsibility for our existence if we will face up to it. Anxiety in the face of death,

Heidegger explains, 'liberates [Dasein] from possibilities which "count for nothing", and lets [Dasein] become free *for* those which are authentic' (*Being and Time*, p. 395).

I say '*if* we face up to', because a fundamental feature of human existence is that, although we know with certainty that it will someday end, we adopt a variety of strategies to avoid having to confront the consequences of this fact. Death is a possibility for each of us. In fact, it is not just any possibility; 'death is Dasein's ownmost possibility'. This means that it is death which makes us the beings that we are. We are distinguished from the gods by our mortality. We are distinguished from animals and other living creatures by the fact that we *experience* ourselves as mortal. The experience of death is, then, an essential distinguishing mark of what it is to be human. The nature of human life and the nature of human death are tied inextricably together.

To think through the existential consequences of our mortality − to ask how death shapes and guides the way we humans exist, the way we live our lives − we must first arrive at a correct conception of the nature of death. When it comes to thinking about death, Heidegger believes that we tend to overlook its existential importance because we typically mistake the cause of death with its essence. In Heidegger's terminology, we focus on our 'demise' rather than our death. The distinction between 'death' and 'demise' is, in other words, a distinction between the existential significance of an event, and the causal or logical or social or legal causes and consequences of the event.

The same distinction could be made with respect to any significant event in human life; to illustrate, let's take one such event − marriage. There are lots of different ways we could pick out or identify marriage. We could describe it in terms of the procedures involved in entering into marriage (put roughly, marriage is the event at which two parties reciprocally contract to live with and support one another during their joint lives). We could describe it in terms of its legal consequences (for example, the change in tax status that comes with marriage, or the alteration of inheritance rights, or the way that a man acquires paternal rights over the children of his spouse), or its social consequences (for example, the social improprieties involved in flirting with a married woman, or inviting a man but not his spouse to a social affair). All of these ways of talking about marriage would succeed in (at least partially) identifying it, and illuminating its causes and effects. But none of them would get directly to the heart of marriage – that is, what it is like to be a married person. To describe this, we would want to know how marriage changes our understanding and self-interpretation (the projects we have), our disposedness (the way things matter to us), and the kind of activities and objects we find ourselves preoccupied with.

In the same way, Heidegger thinks, if we are preoccupied with the events associated with death, we will miss the core existential structure of death, namely, the way that death gives shape and structure to our existence. We could talk about the physical causes of death – perhaps 'the cessation of breathing and heartbeat'. Or we could talk about the legal consequences of death (say, the change in legal title to property, or criminal culpability for causing a death). But, while such considerations might indirectly show us how death shapes our existence, they wouldn't get to the heart of the matter. What we are after is not what events occur at the moment of dying, but the existential *consequences* of those events.

To keep our discussion of death straight, then, we need first to keep straight the distinction between the events that produce the condition of death, and the condition itself. We will follow Heidegger by referring to the condition as 'death'.

The events that bring death about, in turn, can be thought of in at least two ways. They can be understood as physical or biological events, in which case we will refer to them as a 'demise'. Or, they can be understood as an existential event, a change in one's mode of being. In that case, we will refer to the event as 'dying': dying is 'Dasein's going-out-of-the-world' (*Being and Time*, p. 285), or 'losing being-in-the-world' (*Being and Time*, p. 281). It might well be that the event of one's demise is identical with the event of one's dying because one way to lose my being-in-the-world is for my body to stop functioning.[6] In addition, demise obviously has existential consequences – when one's heart stops beating, or when one is terminally ill, this obviously affects how one is able to live and act and relate to other things in the world.[7] That would explain why we so often fall to talking about biological and physical events when the death of a human being is at issue (we are concerned to know how she 'died' – i.e., demised – or whether the attending physician could have done anything to prevent her demise). For Heidegger, however, the focus on our demise is simply a way to avoid facing up to the existential significance of death and dying because, after all, physical events are something we can at least try to counteract, whereas existential death is not. We can watch our cholesterol, exercise, quit smoking, and so on – all in an effort to stave off our demise. No doubt it is good to do this, but if healthy living allows us to ignore the inevitability of existential death, then it will actually stand in the way of helping us to live authentically.

What kind of condition is existential death? We can start by thinking about the existential consequences of our demise or of dying. These include no longer being able to act, think, experience or otherwise be in the world. If death were actualized, it would be impossible to do anything with anything. But death is a condition which is not now actual and, in fact, is not something that, for the one who dies, could be actual. Thus, Heidegger defines death as 'the possibility of the impossibility of every way of comporting oneself towards anything'. His more full, 'existential-ontological' characterization (that is, a characterization in terms of its structure and significance for our way of being in the world) specifies in what way death shapes our experience of the world: death is a possibility that is *non-relational, certain, indefinite*, and not to be *surpassed* (*Being and Time*, p. 303). It is not to be surpassed because it is impending and inevitable. It is indefinite in the sense that we don't know for certain when it will become impossible to be here, but it could occur at any moment. It is certain, not because we can prove that death will come to us, but because the possibility of death shapes our experience of everything in the world. And it is non-relational because it shows that our relations to other things and people do not ultimately make us who we are. So far in this book, we have reviewed Heidegger's arguments that are meant to show the degree to which our existence is shaped by our relationships with other Daseins and things in the world. Death, as we will see, introduces an important qualification to this claim – we are constituted by the world, but we are never fully and inescapably determined by the world.

There is a perfectly obvious and banal sense in which death is a possibility for each of us, because dying or demise are events which, at any given moment, have a probability of occurring that is greater than 0%. But death is a special possibility – not just because we all die, or because, 'on a long enough time line', the probability of dying rises to 100%. It is because death is the possibility which makes us what we are, it is our 'ownmost' possibility. Let's briefly contrast Heidegger's views with another philosophical account of death. Around 300 BC, Epicurus, the founder of Epicureanism, argued that death, 'that most frightful of evils . . . is nothing to us, seeing that when we exist death is not present, and when death is present we do not exist' (Long and Sedley, p. 150). As a consequence, Epicurus believed that it was incoherent to have anything but a stance of indifference towards our own deaths. For Heidegger, by contrast, death is not 'nothing to us', but our ownmost possibility. And for Heidegger, anxiety in the face of death is the right way to respond to it.

Epicurus's argument follows something like these steps:

1 Something can matter to us only if we can experience it.
2 We can experience something if and only if we exist when it is present.
3 We do not exist when (our) death is present.
4 Therefore, we cannot experience death (2, 3).
5 Therefore, death cannot matter to us (1, 4).

This argument seems to work to the extent that we think of death as an ordinary physical entity or event. It seems true that I can't experience particular objects or events – say, this picture of my wife on my desk – unless I exist when it is present. At the same time, Epicurus's conclusion seems absurd: of course my death matters to me. Heidegger's view of death helps us understand where Epicurus's argument goes wrong.

For Epicurus, 'being present to' means something like 'being in (the right kind of) causal contact with . . .' But 'being present' doesn't always requires actual causal contact. Some things are present to us even when they are not exercising a causal impact on us. Consider, for example, a condition like blindness. Blindness can be 'present to me' without my being in causal contact with any particular object or event. Blindness is 'present to me' when I lack the ability to interact with objects in a visual way. So the class of things that are present to me needs to include not just objects that are causally acting on me, but also conditions like blindness – conditions that need to be understood as a mode of access to or receptivity to objects. Blindness is a way of being that shapes the possibilities that are open to me – it excludes me from the possibility of visually experiencing the world (although it may open up possibilities for hearing or smelling or feeling the world that are not normally available to people with sight). A particular way of being receptive to things is 'present to me' when it shapes my possibilities for relating to objects.

Of course death is not like blindness in the sense that death is not something I can experience while in that condition (see Epicurus's premise 3). But we've learned an important lesson all the same: something can matter to me not simply when it is an object that is physically impacting me, but also when it shapes and affects the way I exist in the world.

The next question is whether something can shape and affect my experience of the world, even when it is not something actual (like blindness), but something possible. The answer is 'yes': when we 'have possibilities', they shape our experience of the world. Suppose I know that there is a possibility that a friend will pay me a visit this afternoon. Having this possibility makes me keenly aware of the disarray in my home and the lack of anything suitable to serve a visiting guest. Things of which I would otherwise have been oblivious are made suddenly prominent. The fact that we don't exist when death is actual is thus irrelevant. We do exist when death is possible, and this possibility changes not just our awareness of certain things in the world, but the significance of those things. So Heidegger agrees with Epicurus's premise three: 'Death, as possibility, gives Dasein nothing to be "actualized", nothing which Dasein, as actual, could itself be.' But our death is present to us as a possibility nonetheless, and it matters to us that we might not be able to comport ourselves towards things any more, even if we can't experience being unable to do so. If this is true, then Epicurus is wrong – death is not nothing to us.

Let's look a little more carefully at the idea of having a possibility present to us. There is a difference between having a possibility, and having the possibility present to us *as* a possibility. I can have a possibility without having the slightest intimation of it, without it changing in the least my experience of things. There is probably some mathematical chance that I will be struck by a meteor this afternoon, but the likelihood is so small that I never give it a thought. It is not present to me as a possibility: the minor probability of being killed by a meteor does not affect how I act in the slightest. By contrast, a possibility is present *as* a possibility for me when it shapes the meaning of the situation that I now find myself in. When I am driving my car on Highway 89, there is an ever-present possibility that another vehicle will collide with me. This possibility is present to me, even if I am not thinking about it or brooding over it, because it shapes lots of things I do in my car – my use of turn signals, my driving in the slow lane, my checking my mirrors before changing lanes, and so on. The possibility is present to me *as* a possibility, by determining the significance of the things I encounter and the actions I perform.

In the same way, death is present to me if it shapes the meaning of the situations I find myself in and guides the kinds of actions I perform in those situations. How does death shape our existence? Heidegger's answer is: death 'individualizes Dasein down to itself. This individualizing is a way in which my situation is disclosed for existence. It makes manifest that all being-alongside the things with which we concern ourselves, and all being-with others, will fail us when our own-most potentiality-for-being is at issue.' The possibility of death, in other words, shows my world as the kind of place in which no way of being will be ultimately successful, no way of being will allow me to continue being who I am.[8] This recognition, Heidegger believes, should shatter our reliance on cultural norms and practices, which purport to give us *the* right way to live. Coming to terms with death, then, allows us to take responsibility for ourselves.

For this reason, Heidegger argues that the authentic response to death is 'anticipation'. 'Anticipation . . ., unlike inauthentic being-towards-death, does not evade the fact that death is not to be outstripped; instead, anticipation frees itself for accepting this.' 'Anticipation of death', *Vorlaufen in den Tod*, could more accurately and literally be translated as 'running ahead into death'. One advantage of the metaphor of running is that it suggests our relationship to death is more than a mere mental state. If having our death present to us as a possibility meant it constantly weighed on our thoughts, Heidegger's view would be pretty gloomy. He would be suggesting that we ought to constantly brood over our inevitable death. But, as Heidegger notes, such brooding and reflecting on death, par-adoxically, often arises from the desire to stave off death, to deny it as a possibility (see *Being and Time*, pp. 305–6).

Fortunately, what he has in mind is quite different. Heidegger suggests that we allow our relations to things and to other people to appear in the light of the inevitability of dying. In advocating a running *ahead* towards death, I think Heidegger wants us to picture our stance towards death as a way of being in the world that takes us out and away from the pack, away from the conventional, public, inauthentic norms of the 'one' (*das Man*). When we orient our lives towards death, we find our existence 'wrenched . . . away from the "they"', because we recognize that shared conventions or norms will ultimately fail us. They might get us through everyday situations for the time being, but they ultimately can't help preserve our way of being in the world: death 'makes manifest that all being-alongside the things with which we concern ourselves and all being-with others, will fail us when our ownmost ability to be is the issue'.

For Heidegger, 'death lays claim to [Dasein] as an individual' and 'individualizes Dasein down to itself'. What others say I should do or think I should do is, in the face of death, revealed as irrelevant. This is the non-relationality of death – in it, my relations to the other people around me are thus severed, and I am revealed as not ultimately dependent on the others around me. In anticipating death, I take responsibility for myself. I become authentic, my own person, meaning that I accept that my decisions are not required or essential, because there is no right way to be a human being. As a consequence of my anxiety in the face of death, I am set free to live my life as my own rather than doing things merely because others expect me to do them.

Because it makes it possible to be authentic, Heidegger believes that death is not in and of itself to be resented and avoided. Indeed, far from interfering with life, anxiety in the face of death brings 'an unshakable joy' (*Being and Time*, p. 358). After all, the fact that our lives will end only gives that much more weight and significance to the particular choices that we make in life.

7

TRUTH AND ART

Setting up a world and setting forth the earth, the work [of art] is the instigation of the strife in which the unconcealment of beings as a whole, or truth, is won.

Truth happens [for example] in the [Greek] temple's standing where it is. This does not mean that something is correctly represented and rendered here, but that beings as a whole are brought into unconcealment and held therein. To hold originally means to take into protective heed. Truth happens in Van Gogh's painting [of a peasant's shoes]. This does not mean that something at hand is correctly portrayed but rather that in the revelation of the equipmental being of the shoes, beings as a whole — world and earth in their counterplay — attain to unconcealment. Thus in the work it is truth, not merely something true, that is at work. The picture that shows the peasant shoes, the poem that says the Roman fountain, do not simply make manifest what these isolated beings as such are — if indeed they manifest anything at all; rather, they make unconcealment as such happen in regard to beings as a whole. The more simply and essentially the shoes are engrossed in their essence, the more directly and engagingly do all beings attain a greater degree of being along with them. That is how self-concealing being is cleared. Light of this kind joins its shining to and into the work. This shining, joined in the work, is the beautiful. *Beauty is one way in which truth essentially occurs as unconcealment.* ('The Origin of the Work of Art', in *Basic Writings*, pp. 180–81)

The rest of the chapters in this volume look primarily at Heidegger's later essays. In his works in the 1930s and after, Heidegger was less interested in uncovering static, universal structures of being, and more concerned to understand the contemporary historical situation. Germany in the 1930s, of course, was undergoing considerable upheaval. In the aftermath of the First World War, Germany experienced a political revolution, economic crises, political humiliation and the rise of nationalist and anti-modernist movements like National Socialism. Many in Germany had the sense that Germany, and indeed the whole Western world, was at the brink of a world-historical change.

Heidegger, like many other leading intellectuals of the time, turned his attention to the nature of the historical moment. The passage above comes from 'The Origin of the Work of Art', one of the formative essays that marked the change in Heidegger's approach to philosophy. His thought in this period turned increasingly to understanding how different 'worlds come to pass and founder' (*Beiträge zur Philosophie*, p. 476). A world 'comes to pass' when things are uncovered in a new way and organized differently into a meaningful whole. Great works of art, Heidegger argued, can play an important role in establishing a world. They do this by letting the truth be seen.

Many would deny that art works are concerned with showing the truth. They seem rather to be interested in artful illusion. Or if a work of art is true, that means that it correctly or realistically represents an object in picture or sculpture. For Heidegger, the 'truth' of art is not a matter of a correctness or accuracy in representation, but consists in showing us what things really are. To do this, the art work doesn't need to realistically represent something. 'Truth happens' in the work of art, but 'this does not mean that something is correctly represented and rendered here, but that beings as a whole are brought into unconcealment and held therein'. Heidegger's use of the word 'truth' in these passages contrasts sharply with the way most philosophers in the analytical tradition use the term. Starting with Frege's founding works in analytical philosophy, it has been commonplace to treat only things like assertions or beliefs as capable of being true or false. Such things are true or false by 'correctly representing' or 'agreeing with' or 'corresponding to' some fact or state of affairs. Heidegger does not deny that this is one perfectly legitimate way of using the word 'truth'. Nor does he dispute that an assertion or a belief is true if and only if it agrees with or corresponds with the way things are. But he does deny that the truth of assertions and beliefs is the only, or even the most important kind of truth.

Heidegger is quick to point out that we use the word 'true' to refer to all kinds of things besides assertions and beliefs. We say things like 'he is a true friend'. A friend isn't true because he agrees with the way things are, and a false friend is just as real as a true one. His act of betrayal is a fact (no matter how much he may wish to deceive you about it). A true friend is the one whose friendly actions show him as he really is. The false friend doesn't really show himself in his words and deeds, but conceals his true intentions. Heidegger calls this kind of truth 'ontic truth' or 'the uncoveredness' of entities. Assertions and beliefs play a role in the 'truth' – i.e., the uncovering or making manifest – of entities by helping us to see things as they really are. But entities are best uncovered when we can do more than merely talk about them – when we have practices and skills for dealing with them in the appropriate manner. A chair is most clearly uncovered as a chair, for example, by the simple act of sitting on it. The action shows the 'truth' about the chair more clearly and convincingly than an endless amount of chatter about it.

In addition, what we say or believe about an object can only be true or false if there is a way that the object is in itself. Heidegger argues as a result that the truth of assertions is less fundamental then the ontic truth in which things show themselves as they are in themselves. It is only when an entity is uncovered in our skilful dealings with the world, Heidegger argues, that 'we can make assertions about it and also check them . . . Only because the entity itself is true [i.e., uncovered] can propositions about the entity be true in a derived sense' (*Einleitung in die Philosophie*, p. 78). Unless things show themselves to us as they really are, it is not possible for our assertions and beliefs to agree with the way things are.

One might now wonder: 'What is truth in general? What do true beliefs and true friends have in common?' Heidegger's answer is that truth is 'unconcealment'. True assertions bring a state of affairs out of concealment, and let us focus on and discover the implications of a certain part of the world. True friends show us their nature as human beings, and let us relate to them and interact with them as such. In his later work, Heidegger argues that things and states of affairs can only be brought out of concealment or shown for what they are if the world as a whole is also unconcealed (see "The Origin of the Work of Art', p. 177).

Heidegger believes that the world as a whole is shown to us through the work of art. The work of art, Heidegger explains, 'is the instigation of the strife in which the unconcealment of beings as a whole . . . is won'. A work of art like Van Gogh's *A Pair of Shoes* is not concerned with 'correctly portraying' some entity, but rather it brings about a 'revelation of the equipmental being of the shoes'. Works of art, like phenomenological descriptions, thus unconceal entities for us by helping us to see what those things really are. But the work of art isn't really concerned with helping us to use things more efficiently. It is not as if we consult Van Gogh's painting to learn how we are supposed to wear shoes. Instead, the work of art depicts entities in such a way that 'beings as a whole, world and earth in their counterplay attain to unconcealment'. Heidegger believes, in other words, that a work of art can show us an entity, and shows it so purely and beautifully that by learning to see and feel the work of art, we also are in a position to understand and uncover entities as a whole, as they show up in a specific historical world. By giving us a sense for the peasant's world through her shoes, Van Gogh teaches us to see all the other things that belong to that world as well.

Works of art help us to grasp the character of a world, Heidegger claims, by 'instigating' a struggle or fight between 'earth' and 'world'. 'World' in 'The Origin of the Work of Art' names, by and large, the same thing it did in *Being and Time*. It is not itself an object, the sum of all objects, nor is it an idea or abstraction drawn from objects:

> The world is not the mere collection of the countable or uncountable, familiar and unfamiliar things that are at hand. But neither is it a merely imagined framework added by our representation to the sum of such given things ... World is never an object that stands before us and can be seen. World is the ever-nonobjective to which we are subject as long as the paths of birth and death, blessing and curse keep us transported into being. ('The Origin of the Work of Art', p. 170)

Thus, the world is the unified and coherent whole that structures our relations to the people and things around us, even as it structures the way that things and activities line up with and refer to each other (see chapter 2). In this essay, Heidegger defines the world as 'the clearing of the paths of the essential guiding directions with which all decision complies' ('The Origin of the Work of Art', p. 180). All the particular decisions I make – whether to watch TV or go to the symphony, whether to be a writer or an attorney – are possible only because the world has opened up those possibilities for me. The world makes 'paths' that direct our decisions, but that is not all. It also establishes norms according to which some decisions are more important than others, some options more praiseworthy than others, and so on.

In ordinary usage, the word 'earth' can be either used synonymously with 'world' to refer to this planet, or it can be used as a 'mass noun', meaning that it names an undifferentiated quantity of stuff or substance (soil). As a first crude and potentially misleading approximation one can take the word 'earth' in this essay as also functioning as a mass noun, naming the matter or substance from which all the particular entities in the world are drawn. All the perceivable entities in the world are entities of the earth. The idea is something like this: world, the intelligible ordering of things, settles into the matter or substance out of which everything is drawn. That means that the world's way of making sense of the world actually gives shape and order to all the things within the world. The earth contributes the materiality of things and, in so doing, allows all the worldly entities with which we deal to arise. This is a useful way to start thinking about earth, but it has one serious problem. When we describe earth as the 'matter' or 'substance' out of which everything is formed, we are invoking pre-existing notions of what matter or substance is. 'Matter', the stuff or material out of which something is made, is a concept that originates with Aristotle's distinction between matter and form in the fourth century BC. Aristotle and the Greeks experienced the earth as the material that resists but also supports the forms we impose on things. 'Substance' was a central concept in scholastic philosophy, and names what subsists or 'stands under' all the changing appearances of an object. The substance is what subsists by itself, and requires nothing else to support it. Properties like colour, by contrast, need to exist in something else – in a substance. For the philosophical tradition that developed the notion of substances, the earth was experienced as something that lacks any properties of its own, but supports or 'stands under' all the properties of a thing. By the time Berkeley was writing *Three Dialogues between Hylas and Philonous* in the early eighteenth century, however, this idea which had once seemed so natural and self-evident came to seem absurd. 'I once thought I understood well enough,' one of Berkeley's characters declares, what it means for a substance to support accidents. 'But now,' he continues, 'the more I think on it the less can I comprehend it: in short I find that I know nothing of it.'

If we define the earth as the matter or substance of things, we will be using ideas which themselves are artefacts of particular worlds, with their own specific ways of making things intelligible. But we want a notion of 'earth' that explains what supports all the different worlds. Obviously, then, our concept of earth cannot be naively adopted from the concepts appropriate to just one of those worlds.

For Heidegger, there are two fundamental features of the earth: it emerges into all the entities in the world, and it shelters and supports those entities and the practices and activities that involve them. Of the shelter and support that the earth provides, Heidegger writes: 'The earth is that whither the rising up (*Aufgehen*) of all that rises up is brought back into shelter, and indeed sheltered as something rising up' ('The Origin of the Work of Art', p. 168, translation modified).

One of the uses of the German verb '*aufgehen*' – the main usage that Heidegger draws on here – is to describe the sprouting or shooting forth of plants. The earth gives its substance to the plants that shoot forth from it: they are grown out of the earth in both the spatial sense that they come from out of the earth, and also in the material sense that they are made up of or consist of earth. At the same time, the earth protects and shelters those plants by letting them root back into the earth. In a precisely analogous way, all worldly things arise from and are sheltered in the earth by going back into the earth. Indeed, in a contemporaneous book manuscript, Heidegger even describes the way the earth shelters the world by allowing our habitual practices to 'grow back into the closedness of the earth. This growing back never enacts itself in a mere representing and feeling, but rather always in taking care of, making, working, in short in letting the world world' (*Beiträge zur Philosophie*, p. 391). Our practices, just like plants, need to settle back into something dark, something that we don't need to think about or pay attention to. Think of what it is like to learn a new skill like eating with chopsticks. When one first tries it, one is very conscious of the feel of the chopsticks, the awkward position of one's hands, the new-found slipperiness of chunks of food. And yet, with practice, all of the things the beginner is so conscious of disappear, settling back into unobtrusiveness. In fact, all our practices are like this. As we become skilful at anything, our ability settles into our bodies and roots itself in the equipment we use so that, like the roots of a plant, our bodily dispositions and the equipment we use support our actions inconspicuously.

Letting the world 'world' means letting it arrange and organize and make coherent and relate all the entities in the world. We do this by actually dealing with the entities around us – by making them, working with them, caring for them.

As we deal with entities, we inevitably experience something that exceeds our control, dictating limits to how they can actually be arranged or used. This is the earth 'rising up' into the worldly things, sustaining them but also setting conditions on their use. As a trivial example of 'earthy' sustaining and limiting, think of the impact that gravity has on our ability to play football. Without gravity, it would be impossible to play the game at all – one unblocked kick, and the ball would go sailing off for ever. But at the same time, gravity limits what the players can do. Even the greatest player can only jump so high, leap so far. Similarly, a world as a whole, as we've seen, tries to establish a style that governs all entities and activities in a uniform way. In the medieval world, for instance, everything was understood in terms of its nearness to or distance from God. The 'worlding' of the medieval world can be readily seen in medieval cathedrals, whose very stones strive for divinity as they soar above the earth towards the heavens, and open up expanses of windows to allow the celestial light to shine into the building. The earthiness of the stones supported this world by allowing the cathedrals to be built, but it also limited the world by setting constraints on what could be done with the stones. When those limits were exceeded, and they often were, the result was catastrophic, as buildings would collapse and bring down with them the efforts and aspirations of generations of faithful workers.

As a world strives to grow back into the earth, it encounters resistance. In the process, the earth appears in a determinate way in terms of the resistance that the world encounters. In building the cathedral, we discover particular ways in which our practices are limited and constrained. These are different limits and constraints than we discover when we are building a different kind of building, where delicate stone traceries and large stained-glass windows are unnecessary. 'In essential strife,'

Heidegger notes, 'the opponents raise each other into the self-assertion of their essence' ('The Origin of the Work of Art', p. 174, translation modified). Both world and earth appear in the light of the way they impose conditions and constraints on each other.

Heidegger's description of the earth is carefully crafted to avoid attributing to the earth any particular, world-specific understanding of what it is. In fact, it goes further than this: in talking about the 'closedness' of the earth, Heidegger's precise point is that the earth upon which the world is grounded cannot be understood and determinately conceptualized. This isn't a bad thing. In fact, it is precisely because there are things we can't get clear about, but that simply act on us immediately and directly, that our decisions have gravity and weight. Our worlds, and consequently our meaningful relations to things, are always based in something that can't be explained in terms of the prevailing intelligible structure of the world: 'The world is the clearing of the paths of the essential guiding directions with which all decision complies. Every decision, however, bases itself on something not mastered, something concealed, confusing; else it would never be a decision' ('The Origin of the Work of Art', p. 180). Think, for example, about the way the modern world strives to reorganize things to make them as available for us as possible, and to allow us to master and control them as much as possible. As a result, moderns understand the being of entities in the world in terms of their causal structures, because it is knowledge of these structures that allows us best to master and control them. But why are we so driven to reorganize the world to facilitate our mastery? The existence of other worlds, worlds destroyed by the modern drive for mastery and control, shows that it is not a natural and self-evident proposition that the world should be organized in such a way as to maximize control. That some prefer the modern world to, say, the premodern world of nineteenth-century Japan doesn't resolve the issue – it simply focuses it. One might argue, for example, that the modernization and industrialization of Japan were desirable because they brought a higher gross domestic product and per capita income, even if they came at the expense of traditional forms of life, leading to changes in diet, in housing and in kinds of vocations, and to exploitation and degradation of the environment.[9] But increasing the gross domestic product or per capita income are only good reasons for industrializing the country to the extent that one prefers an increase in average wealth to the features of life that are sacrificed with modernization. But why one should have just those preferences is precisely what is at issue – if one would prefer the pace and style of premodern Japanese life to an increase of per capita income, then the argument that Japan should modernize in order to increase average income will not be persuasive. Ultimately, the issue was decided not by argument, but by force; just as one would expect where it is the most basic sense for what is worth pursuing that is at issue.

So it seems that the strength of the drive to establish a new world and destroy the old depends on something withdrawing from view – that is, becoming so self-evident that it is no longer open to question: namely, the desirability of the new world itself. This desirability is an earthly thing: it withdraws and shelters the world it supports. If it didn't withdraw by becoming so obvious that we no longer think much about it, let alone question it, it would not be capable of supporting the world that is organized on its basis. Imagine, for example, that our culture had a genuine question about the desirability of making everything as flexible and efficient as possible. We would have a genuine debate over whether to use every new technological innovation, one in which we couldn't appeal to increases in efficiency as a justification for employing the technology. Indeed, it is likely that we would not devote so much energy and expense to developing technological innovations in the first place, so the debate would be unlikely ever to arise. Contrast this with the debates we actually have over technological innovations. These tend to turn on the question of whether we have properly weighed all of the costs against the benefits; that we should want the most efficient way to deal with the world is not itself open to debate. Our world is supported by our most basic preference – a taste for efficiency and flexibility – having largely withdrawn from view.

It is this self-closing but sheltering that characterizes the earth as earth, not its possession of any particular material properties. 'The earth is the spontaneous forthcoming of that which is continually self-secluding and to that extent sheltering and concealing' ('The Origin of the Work of Art', p. 174). At this point, some might be tempted to throw up their hands in frustration and cry 'Why can't Heidegger just tell me *what* the earth is.' This question is looking for a way of making things intelligible independently of any world. But Heidegger's point is that there is no such world-transcendent perspective from which to understand things. Whenever we understand anything, our understanding is based in our world, and built on the foundation of the withdrawal of the earth. If we specify what the earth is, then, we will only be naming how it appears relative to our experience of the world. But that shouldn't lead you to think that 'earth' is an abstraction. There always is something resisting and supporting our practices, and that something is very real.

The work of art provokes a struggle between earth and world, by helping to establish a coherent style or way of being that can govern how everything appears. The work of art is itself a place where the struggle occurs. It 'sets up' the world and 'sets forth' the earth – that is, it allows each to have a determinate enough form that they *can* come into conflict with one another. The role of the great works of art is to make a world possible by letting a certain style for organizing things shine and attune us to them. It sets up a style and draws us to it. This style or way of inhabiting the world is so beautifully depicted that we feel attracted to it, even if (or, perhaps precisely because) we can't understand it. Each work of art lets a particular thing – for example, shoes, or a building – be seen as it appears within that world. The art work shows us the essence of the thing purely and simply, so free of distraction or adornment that we can see what is really at stake in the world and, perhaps, be drawn to it. The work, in other words, lets some entity shine, appear as beautiful, and thus bring us to feel the world differently. It is only when something shines and appears as beautiful that we are drawn to start engaging in the practices that will let the new world settle into the earth.

Of course, works of art are not the only things which can 'shine', that is, hold up a new way or style of existing that draws us to it. Heidegger suggested that another way to create a new truth of being occurs in 'the thinker's questioning', that is, through a philosopher articulating a new style for making sense of the world. Other ways include things like 'the act that founds a political state' and 'the essential sacrifice' ('The Origin of the Work of Art', pp. 186–7). When he writes about these in Germany in 1935–6, it is clear that Heidegger has in mind the National Socialist revolution which had given Hitler absolute power in Germany and led to the establishment of a new National Socialist state.

Heidegger was appointed rector of Freiburg University and joined the National Socialist German Workers' Party in 1933, the year that saw Hitler become chancellor and the Reichstag pass the Enabling Act that allowed Hitler to seize absolute power in Germany. Heidegger resigned the rectorship in 1934, but not before becoming intensely involved with the

Nazi Party's programme of university reform. The Nazis set out to reorganize all of German life, the universities included; Heidegger hoped to take advantage of the opportunity to implement for Freiburg his vision of the relationship between philosophy and the sciences in German universities (see Thomson 2005A, pp. 32–4). Heidegger was also attracted by the Nazi Party's anti-modernism, which he hoped would allow Germany to realize a non-technological style for organizing everyday life. Heidegger later admitted that his 'hopes for Hitler' were 'badly disappointed', as were his ambitions of helping to develop National Socialism in a more philosophical direction (see *Reden*, p. 697). Even his ambitions for university reform were frustrated. For his support of the National Socialist regime while rector, Heidegger was banned from teaching by the Denazification Commission following the war.

His public addresses while rector of Freiburg University give us some clues to interpret his claim that an essential sacrifice can disclose a new world. If we ignore the historical context of Nazi Germany, the 'essential sacrifice' could refer to any act in which one gives up one's life or being for a cause, for example Jesus's self-sacrifice on the cross, which opened up the Christian world (see Dreyfus, 'Heidegger's Ontology of Art'). But the historical context is hard to ignore. In public addresses roughly contemporaneous with his writing of 'The Origin of the Work of Art', Heidegger repeatedly employed the National Socialist rhetoric of martyrdom. He exhorted the students of Freiburg University to sacrifice themselves for the nation in the spirit of the student-soldiers who had been slaughtered at the battle of Langemarck (Ypern) in 1914 (see 'Der Deutsche Student als Arbeiter', in *Reden*, p. 197). According to legend, the German youth of Langemarck had charged to their deaths singing 'Deutschland, Deutschland über alles'. Heidegger also frequently idealized the sacrifice of Albert Leo Schlageter, an early member and hero of the Nazi Party who had been executed by the French in 1923 for sabotage during the French occupation of the Ruhr (see 'Zur Immatrikulation', in *Reden*, p. 97; 'Der Deutsche Student als Arbeiter', p. 207; or 'Gedenkworte zu Schlageter', in *Reden*, pp. 759-60). Heidegger also praised the 'highest sacrifice' offered by the frontline soldiers of the Great War on behalf of the German people (see '25 Jahre nach unserem abiturium', in *Reden*, p. 279; see also *Hölderlins Hymnen 'Germanien' und 'Der Rhein'*, pp. 72–3). From all this it is clear that he saw sacrifice on behalf of the new National Socialist state as just the kind of a world-disclosive sacrifice that he describes in 'The Origin of the Work of Art'. As he explained in a public lecture entitled 'The University in the National Socialist State', 'we contemporary ones stand in the struggle for a new reality. We are only a passage, only a sacrifice' ('Die Universität im National-sozialistischen Staat', in *Reden*, p. 765).

The acts of the Nazi leaders and heroes, in other words, were examples for Heidegger of shining deeds – acts attracting and motivating a people to reconfigure their practices and change their dispositions for the world. Heidegger mistakenly believed that the National Socialist revolution presented an opportunity for the German people to head off the worst features of modernism, which were disrupting and threatening traditional forms of German life (that Heidegger was not alone in making this mistake, of course, hardly excuses him of responsibility for supporting the regime). As we'll see in chapter 9, Heidegger thought that the technological style of the modern world leads to a reduction of everything, including human beings, into mere resources, posing a grave threat to our ability to live worthwhile lives.

Heidegger's account of works of art helps explain his

susceptibility to the lure of National Socialism. He saw in Nazism the chance to change the current configuration of the world, tearing Germany out of modernism and opening up new possibilities for existence. Because the earth, the basis for the decisions that ground a new world cannot be made clear – indeed, must close itself off in order to govern the new world – those who are drawn to a new work of art or other shining deeds, and who 'transform entities' in the light of the work (see *Beiträge zur Philosophie*, p. 96), will always be susceptible to the danger that the resulting world is more horrific than the current mode of existence. It is reprehensible that Heidegger seems not to have been more cognizant of this danger.

For many philosophers, Heidegger's involvement with National Socialism has offered a good reason (or at least an excuse) to ignore his work. For students of Heidegger, his terrible mistake is a sobering reminder of the serious consequences of his thought, and any responsible follower of Heidegger needs to come to terms with it. It is disconcerting, to say the least, that Heidegger, who purported to have unique insight into the movement of world history, proved to be so terribly blind to the significance of the events that played out before his eyes. It is downright distressing to see how poorly Heidegger behaved in the circumstances – while there is little evidence that Heidegger was himself anti-Semitic, for example, he was not above exploiting the prevailing anti-Semitism when it served his purposes. It is not surprising, then, that one of the most hotly debated issues in Heidegger scholarship is the question of what lessons should be learned from Heidegger's involvement with the Nazi Party (for an overview of the different strategies for dealing with Heidegger's Nazism, see Thomson, 'Heidegger and National Socialism').

While he never abandoned the fundamental idea that worlds are opened up in ways that resist clarity and rational grounding, Heidegger's work after the war did go some way towards overcoming the political naivete that led to his disastrous involvement with National Socialism. He did this by, first, getting much clearer than he had been about the dangers of the modern world – the dangers which led him to think we need a new world disclosure. Once he was able to articulate the danger of modernity in terms of technology, it became clear that National Socialism was just another modern, technological movement (even if it employed technology for reactionary goals). Second, Heidegger abandoned his romantic infatuation with struggle, and mythical political deeds and sacrifices in favour of a more gentle and receptive form of openness to the earth and sky, mortals and divinities.

8

LANGUAGE

Speaking is known as the articulated vocalization of thought by means of the organs of speech. But speaking is at the same time also listening. It is the custom to put speaking and listening in opposition: one man speaks, the other listens. But listening accompanies and surrounds not only speaking such as takes place in conversation. The simultaneousness of speaking and listening has a larger meaning. Speaking is of itself a listening. Speaking is listening to the language which we speak. Thus, it is a listening not *while* but *before* we are speaking. This listening to language also comes before all other kinds of listening that we know, in a most inconspicuous manner. We do not merely speak *the* language – we speak *by way of* it. We can do so solely because we always have already listened to the language. What do we hear there? We hear language speaking.

But – does language itself speak? How is it supposed to perform such a feat when obviously it is not equipped with organs of speech? Yet *language* speaks. Language first of all and inherently obeys the essential nature of speaking: it says. Language speaks by saying, this is, by showing. What it says wells up from the formerly spoken and so far still unspoken Saying which pervades the design (*Aufriss*) of language (*Sprachwesen*). Language speaks in that it, as showing, reaching into all regions of presences, summons from them whatever is present to appear and to fade. We, accordingly,

> listen to language in this way, that we let it say its Saying to
> us. No matter in what way we may listen besides, whenever we
> are listening to something we are *letting something be said to
> us*, and all perception and conception is already contained in
> that act. In our speaking, as a listening to language, we say
> again the Saying we have heard. We let its soundless voice
> come to us, and then demand, reach out and call for the
> sound that is already kept in store for us ('The Way to
> Language', in *On the Way to Language*, pp. 123–4).

For the last century, the analysis of language has been the cor-
nerstone of philosophy in the English-speaking world. As
Oxford philosopher Michael Dummett has explained, so-called
'analytical philosophy' is based on two beliefs: 'the belief, first,
that a philosophical account of thought can be attained through
a philosophical account of language, and secondly, that a com-
prehensive account can only be so attained' (*Origins of Analytical
Philosophy*, p. 4). For the analytical philosopher, the only way to
arrive at philosophical understanding of a thing is through an
analysis of the sentences or words we use to talk about the
thing. And this, in turn, has led to the philosophy of language
taking pride of place in contemporary philosophy.

Heidegger, too, came to believe that reflection on language
is a central task for thinking, but he draws quite different
lessons from his study of language than analytical philosophers do. The analytical philosopher tries to learn about the
structure of our mental states and attitudes by studying the
logical structure of language. Heidegger is not so much interested in the logical structure of language as in the role
different languages play in establishing different styles of being
in the world. For Heidegger, the key feature for understanding language is to focus on our responsiveness to it, that is, the
way that it shapes and guides our understanding of ourselves
and the world around us '*before* we are speaking'.

To illustrate what this means, imagine that I ask you to look out of the window and tell me what you see. As you look at the scene in front of you, certain features leap out as the important ones to describe. As you start to describe it, the words come to you ready made. You are responding in speech to the way the world presents itself as already speak*able*. As Heidegger describes it, 'we speak *by way of* (*aus*)' language – more literally, we speak *from out of* a language, by 'listening' to it and letting 'its soundless voice come to us, and then we desire, reach out, and call for the sound that is already kept in store for us' (translation modified). When we are engaged in conversation, we are also listening to language as manifest by the way the right words to say simply come to us, almost as if by their own accord. But even when we have the experience of words failing us, of language denying itself to us, even then, as we grasp for words, we are listening to what language has to say about the matter.

Speaking originates, then, in something that is independent of our particular intentions, something which shows us the world in such a way that we can speak about it. It is this phenomenon Heidegger has in view when he says that 'speaking is listening to the language which we speak'. Heidegger names the thing that we are listening to 'originary language', or the essence of language (*Wesen der Sprache*), or, in our passage, the 'linguistic essence' (*Sprachwesen*).[10]

The essence of language, according to Heidegger, is the 'saying' that shows things: 'Language speaks by saying, that is, by showing . . . Language speaks in that it, as showing, reaching into all regions of presences, summons from them whatever is present to appear and to fade.' The originary language, then, is the articulation prior to any human speech that makes salient particular features of the world by setting things into a certain structure. It is a kind of pointing out or showing, a highlighting of certain things and not others. The 'saying' of originary language is nothing like an actual vocal articulation. Think again of the phenomenon of having words provided to us as we engage in conversation. We don't actually hear words spoken to us, which we then repeat aloud. Instead, language 'says' by showing us, directing us immediately to what we should say. It silently and inconspicuously draws our attention to what is to be said. As Heidegger sometimes puts it, language is a 'showing saying' – it shows what is there to be spoken about, and thereby allows things to either appear or disappear from view (see 'The Way to Language', p. 126).

Before explaining how language 'says' and 'shows' the world, we need to say more about Heidegger's description of the originary language in terms of 'the essence of language' or the 'linguistic essence'. Phrases of the form 'the X of Y', constructed from the genitive 'of' connecting two nouns, can sometimes be ambiguous – particularly in cases where the first noun implies a verb. Consider, for example, Shakespeare's phrase 'the dread and fear of kings'. This could mean either that kings are feared and dreaded, or, because 'dread' and 'fear' are nouns formed from verbs, that kings fear and dread something. Of course, the context often rules out ambiguity: 'the fear of God' or 'the fear of heights' must mean that someone fears God or heights (God and heights are not the kind of things that can be afraid). Still other such phrases are not ambiguous because the first noun names an entity rather than implying an action: 'the wife of the king' does not have this kind of ambiguity. Normally, an expression like 'the essence of language' would also not be ambiguous, because the noun 'essence' does not imply any action. But Heidegger doesn't use the word 'essence', '*Wesen*', in the normal way: he turns it into a verb.

For Heidegger, 'to essence', means 'to bring something into its essence', where the essence of a thing is what matters to us about it. The essence determines how one appropriately relates to it and the things concerned with it:

> 'It essences' means: it comes to presence, it matters to us enduringly, moves or makes a way for us and concerns us. The essence thought in this manner names that which endures, matters to us in everything because it moves and makes a way for everything. (*Unterwegs zur Sprache*, p. 190)

Obviously, Heidegger is using the term 'essence' in a way unfamiliar to the philosophical tradition. In this tradition, the essence of a thing is the essential property that makes the thing what it is, or the concept by which we grasp what it is. For Heidegger, the essence of a thing is whatever leads us to recognize an essential property or concept as essential. We can illustrate this point with an example. For any particular thing, there is a potentially infinite number of concepts under which to grasp it, because there is an infinite number of properties which it possesses. A piece of gold, for instance, has a colour and a weight and a texture and a shape, but also all sorts of other properties like being good for making bracelets, gleaming in a way that seems divine, being buried in the sand of a riverbed, etc. Which of all these properties are essential to the piece of gold, and which are merely accidental to its being? When we decide what any particular object *is*, and thus decide what its essential properties are, we do so by selecting out from the infinite properties it has some subset that is most important. To do this, we need to have a prior sense for what matters to us and concerns us – we need, in other words, to be disposed to the world in a particular way so that something will appear relevant and important while other things will seem trivial. Something 'essences' in Heidegger's sense when it 'moves us', 'concerns us', 'matters to us in everything'. We disclose the essential properties that we do – the essences of things in the traditional sense – because the Heideggerian essence allows a particular 'character of beings . . . to be ascendent' (*Basic Question of Philosophy*, p. 112) by moving us to be disposed to things in a particular way.

Different domains and worlds will consequently have different Heideggerian essences, and part of inhabiting a world is being moved by the essence proper to the world. This shows us another piece of the traditional view of essences that Heidegger rejects. Traditionally, essences are understood as static, unchanging properties. For Heidegger, which properties are essential will depend on how the Heideggerian essence has oriented us to the world, and thus what is essential about a thing can change historically because different ages or cultures might be 'essenced' differently. For example, one culture might be moved to find things important to the degree that they approach God by being like Him. Another age or culture might find the true being of a thing in what allows it to be turned into a resource, flexibly and efficiently on call for use. When someone disposed to the world in the first way encounters gold, she will take as essential its God-like properties – its incorruptibility, its divine sheen. When someone disposed to the world in the second way encounters gold, she will take the essential property to be whatever it is about it that allows us to most flexibly and efficiently use it as a resource. These, it turns out, are the properties that physics and chemistry focus on: its atomic structure.

Let's now return to the idea of 'the essence of language'. Because 'essence' is for Heidegger a verb, this expression could either refer to the property which makes language what it is (i.e., to language's essential property), or it could refer to language doing something: language essencing. And, in fact, it is the latter implication that Heidegger wants us to focus on in thinking about originary language. The expression 'linguistic essence' in the extract above is meant to rule out the ambiguity. It means simply: language essencing, language bringing things into their essence, language 'moving us' so that things matter to us in a particular kind of way, so that paths are made within which we can move among entities, and so that entities can bear on each other as the entities they are. Language, Heidegger says in another essay, is 'the saying that sets the world into motion' ('*das Welt-bewegende Sage*')' ('Das Wesen der Sprache', in *Unterwegs zur Sprache*, p. 203). Essential language or originary language, it turns out, is what allows different worlds or cultures to be disposed differently, and things to be the kind of things they are for those worlds.

At this point, we need to introduce an important distinction. Heidegger differentiates between the originary language that gives us our most fundamental feel for the world, and our ordinary everyday language we use to communicate with each other about things in the world. The originary language is 'soundless', that is, it 'says' the world without the use of words. Ordinary language speaks only in words. Originary language shows us what is important and unimportant about things, and lets us see how things should be arranged with each other. Ordinary language expresses the facts that originary language lets us see. Originary language speaks by disposing us to the world and, as a consequence, allowing us to see the world lined up and organized in accordance with a particular way of being. Everything, consequently, comes to have a particular essence, to matter to us and move us to respond in particular ways. When we share an orientation to the world with others, we can communicate using the words of ordinary language, because the essencing of originary language makes the same features of the world stand out for both of us as salient, grab our attention, and allow themselves to be referred to by us. We share an originary language when the world is articulated in the same style for us, when we 'listen to language', when 'we let it say its saying to us'. We perform linguistic acts that respond in the right way to the way that the world is articulated when 'we let its soundless voice come to us, and then demand, reach out and call for the sound that is already kept in store for us'.

But what does it mean for originary language to speak to us soundlessly, without words? And how does it manage to organize the world in the process? Originary language doesn't use words or linguistic expressions because it is not concerned with telling us facts, but rather with getting us to feel the world in a particular kind of way. Originary language speaks to us by getting us in the right mood for the world. In a beautiful but neglected essay called 'The Secret of the Bell Tower' ('Vom Geheimnis des Glockenturms', in *Aus der Erfahrung des Denkens*), Heidegger illustrates how this works with an example from his own youth in the village of Messkirch in Baden, a staunchly Catholic area of Germany. Heidegger's father was a sexton, and religious and theological studies played a central role in his early education. Heidegger even entered the Jesuit Novitiate of Tisis, Austria, in the fall of 1909, before being dismissed on health grounds. He eventually broke with 'the *system* of Catholicism', which he came to think of as 'problematic and unacceptable'. But he continued to lecture early in his career on the phenomenology of religion and metaphysics, and later in life returned often in thought to the possibility of experiencing the divine.

As he thought back on the faith of his youth, Heidegger recalled how the church bells articulated the day, the week, and the year into distinct times and seasons. One could hear a certain bell, and be put into the proper mood for a church service. When in that mood, things could show up in the way appropriate for a church service. He recalls how, as a boy, the ringing of the bell tower permeated all his activities, ringing out the hours, the seasons, the holy days, the holy transubstantiation, and punctuating sleep and play, marking out the different moments of the work day. The church bells centred all these diverse activities on the religious services, and gathered the whole world of practices into a coherent whole by linking them to the divine manifestation at the altar. The ringing of the bells, in other words, aligned Heidegger's attunement to the world into a coherence grounded in his experience of the sacred, and allowed him to experience every particular thing in terms of the place it held in a world given meaning and coherence by God's presence. This attunement in which world is given coherence, and things are fixed in their essence, occurs as we pay heed to the sounding of the most originary language.

Once we see things as having a certain significance for us, we will quite naturally use them with other things and in activities suited to the significance they hold. For example, given a medieval Christian's disposition for the world, gold in the Middle Ages might have lined up in a special way with icons, chalices and book covers, because the noble properties of gold were the essential ones and these were best brought out in sacred objects like icons and chalices and Bibles. Today, pictures and cups and books aren't sacred, and the medieval approach to gold is a terribly inefficient use of a valuable resource which, given its properties, is much better used for certain industrial applications. The originary language ends up shaping the style of being of a culture. For this essence to prevail, the relations between beings must be articulated in accordance with that style. Originary language is this articulation, which 'metes out the measure of a being's essence' (see *Unterwegs zur Sprache*, p. 23). In the excerpt above, Heidegger expresses this idea by describing the linguistic essence as a 'design' (an *Aufriss*, a draft or a sketch). The originary language essences by drafting or sketching out in advance what can be experienced, perceived or thought of things.

So the language that Heidegger is talking about is something that speaks to us, as he says in the passage above, '*before* we are speaking'. We speak because we are possessed by language, which means we are oriented to things and regions of the world, in a particular way. When I speak a language, in Heidegger's view – or rather, when a language speaks me – particular things can show themselves to me as having a particular meaning, importance, and relevance to my world. As Heidegger wrote: 'The essence of language comes into its essence there where it occurs as world-forming power, i.e., where it preforms the being of beings in advance and brings them into a contexture' (*Logik als die Frage nach dem Wesen der Sprache*, p. 171). As a result of their different originary languages, for example, the medieval Christian and the modern technophile inhabit different worlds. And that means that their ordinary languages end up being different as well. The word 'gold' names a different thing for a medieval Christian than it does for the technophile. For the technophile, 'gold' names a particularly useful resource. For the medieval, 'gold' names a noble, incorruptible metal.

9

TECHNOLOGY

What is modern technology? It too is a revealing . . . The revealing that rules in modern technology is a challenging, which puts to nature the unreasonable demand that it supply energy which can be extracted and stored as such. But does this not hold true for the old windmill as well? No. Its sails do indeed turn in the wind; they are left entirely to the wind's blowing. But the windmill does not unlock energy from the air currents in order to store it.

In contrast, a tract of land is challenged into the putting out of coal and ore. The earth now reveals itself as a coal mining district, the soil as a mineral deposit. The field that the peasant formerly cultivated and set in order appears differently than it did when to set in order still meant to take care of and maintain. The work of the peasant does not challenge the soil of the field. In sowing grain it places seed in the keeping of the forces of growth and watches over its increase. But meanwhile even the cultivation of the field has come under the grip of another kind of setting-in-order, which *sets* upon nature. It sets upon it in the sense of challenging it. Agriculture is now the mechanized food industry. Air is now set upon to yield nitrogen, the earth to yield ore, ore to yield uranium, for example; uranium is set upon to yield atomic energy, which can be unleashed either for destructive or for peaceful use.

This setting-upon that challenges forth the energies of nature is an expediting, and in two ways. It expedites in that it unlocks and exposes. Yet that expediting is always itself directed from the beginning toward furthering something else, i.e., toward driving on to the maximum yield at the minimum expense. The coal that has been hauled out in some mining district has not been supplied in order that it may simply be present somewhere or other. It is stockpiled; that is, it is on call, ready to deliver the sun's warmth that is stored in it. The sun's warmth is challenged forth for heat, which in turn is ordered to deliver steam whose pressure turns the wheels that keep a factory running . . .

The revealing that rules throughout modern technology has the character of a setting-upon, in the sense of a challenging-forth. That challenging happens in that the energy concealed in nature is unlocked, what is unlocked is transformed, what is transformed is stored up, what is stored up is in turn distributed, and what is distributed is switched about ever anew. Unlocking, transforming, storing, distributing, and switching about are ways of revealing. But the revealing never simply comes to an end. Neither does it run off into the indeterminate. The revealing reveals to itself its own manifoldly interlocking paths, through regulating their course. This regulating itself is, for its part, everywhere secured. Regulating and securing even become the chief characteristics of the challenging revealing.

What kind of unconcealment is it, then, that is peculiar to that which results from this setting-upon that challenges? Everywhere everything is ordered to stand by, to be immediately at hand, indeed to stand there just so that it may be on call for a further ordering. Whatever is ordered about in this way has its own standing. We call it the standing-reserve. The word expresses here something more, and something more essential, than mere 'stock'. The word 'standing-reserve' assumes the rank of an inclusive rubric. It designates nothing less than the way in which everything presences that is wrought upon by the challenging revealing. Whatever stands

by in the sense of standing-reserve no longer stands over
against us as object. ('The Question Concerning Technology',
in *The Question Concerning Technology and Other Essays*,
pp. 14–17)

The first few decades of the twentieth century saw dramatic
changes to traditional modes of life. Industrialization, long
under way in most of Europe and America, revolutionized
agriculture and all the trades in Germany, displacing workers
and leading to mass migrations into cities. With improved
technologies for transportation, local economies were drawn
into national and world markets. New means of communica-
tion led to an increased dissemination of ideas and new forms
of entertainment – film, radio, music – which threatened to
destroy Europe's cultural heritage. Meanwhile, the advance of
the modern sciences in explaining everything naturalistically
was leading to what Max Weber called the disenchantment of
the world, which seemed to hold no more place for spirit,
God or the sacred. Against this background, it is no surprise
that philosophers began to reflect on the nature of technology
in order to try to understand both the threat and the promise
that technology poses for everyday life.

For Heidegger, technology held more threat than promise.
In the last decades of his life, Heidegger lectured repeatedly
and published frequently on technology. His preoccupation
with 'the technological mode of revealing' was driven by the
belief that if we come to experience everything as a mere
resource, our ability to lead worthwhile lives will be put at
risk. His task as a thinker was to awaken us to the danger of
this age, and to point out possible ways for us to avoid the
snares of the technological age.

A central thesis of Heidegger's later work is that there has
been a succession of different worlds, each with its own

essence. These worlds will organize entities into different orders of intelligibility, and thus give their inhabitants very different understandings of how to conduct their lives. In the Christian Middle Ages, for example, everything showed up as God's creation, and was defined in terms of its nearness or distance from God's own nature. Starting in the fifteenth and sixteenth centuries, Western culture entered the modern age in which everything started showing up as either a subject with a deep essence, or an object with fixed properties. Heidegger believed that, with the advent of modern machine technology, modernity began to change in important ways. In the emerging age – the technological age – everything shows up as needing to be reorganized in order to make it more efficient, flexible, useful in an infinite variety of ways.

We can illustrate the difference between these ages by thinking about how differently human being appears for each of them. When someone disposed to the world in the Christian way encounters human beings, she will see them as children of God, and judge them as good or bad to the degree that they submit themselves to God's will. In the Middle Ages, the main categories for understanding humans were 'saints' and 'sinners'. When someone disposed to the world in a technological way encounters human beings, she sees human resources. The good human is the one most flexibly able to deal with shifts in the marketplace, pluralities of cultures, changes in social norms, etc. In their adaptability, human beings in the technological age share a 'style of being' with everything else, because everything is now valued in terms of its flexibility and efficiency.

Modern technology, in other words, has changed our taste or sense for the world. We want everything to be on call, available and ready for use when we want it for whatever purpose we want it. As we search constantly to discover how most

efficiently to rearrange things and realign practices, the significance of things around us changes accordingly. Heidegger
notes that 'the field that the peasant formerly cultivated and set
in order appears differently than it did when to set in order still
meant to take care of and maintain . . . But meanwhile even
the cultivation of the field has come under the grip of another
kind of setting-in-order.' In a previous age, farming practices
reflected a sense that the animals, plants and land were
entrusted to us by God. In such a world, farming could be a
vocation, a call to nurture and care for the land, and not just a
job. The food industry now, by contrast, has been mechanized
and technologized, and there is no longer a sense of steward-
ship over the earth and animals. Instead, we've set out to
improve upon nature, first by breeding, and then by genetic
engineering which 'challenges' nature to do whatever we
want.

In the technological age, what matters to us most is getting
the 'greatest possible use' out of everything.[11] For things to be
maximally usable, they can't have any fixed purposes that constrain what we do with them. Because our relationship to
technologies ends up changing the essence of everything we
encounter, modern technology is dramatically different from
previous technologies. Past ages had their own technologies, of
course, and these also helped people to use things more efficiently. But premodern technologies adapted themselves to the
inherent properties that things had. Modern technology, by contrast, is a 'setting in order that challenges forth the energies of
nature'. (Our translation of this passage has rendered 'to set in
order', 'stellen', as 'setting-upon'. This is somewhat misleading;
the main point is not that technology assaults things, although it
does that too, but that it is a particular way of arranging and
ordering the world.) In challenging nature, technology is an
'expediting, and in two ways. It expedites in that it unlocks and

exposes.' Technology expedites or facilitates our ability to use things in whatever way we want by unlocking, that is, removing things from their natural conditions, and thus freeing them of any properties that might constrain our maximally efficient and flexible use of them. This is what Heidegger is pointing to with the old windmill: 'Its sails do indeed turn in the wind; they are left entirely to the wind's blowing. But the windmill does not unlock energy from the air currents in order to store it.' Modern technology, by contrast, frees itself from the inconvenient dependence of the windmill on the nature of the wind. Technology also facilitates or expedites our maximal use of things in that it 'exposes' – '*herausstellt*', literally, places out into the open – nature. It does this by theoretically grasping things in a way which allows us to unlock them. It opens their secrets up to us so that we can exploit them.

Technology gives us the power to 'transform' objects with fixed properties into resources which are flexible, with no determinate and necessary features or properties. 'What is transformed is stored up', that is, made available for use when-ever and however we might wish. 'What is stored up is in turn distributed, and what is distributed is switched about ever anew.' Heidegger's favourite, and most apt, example of this is electrical power. The properties of a natural resource like coal, which in its natural condition is suitable for burning and pro-viding heat, but not suitable for, to name but a few things, writing books on, or making music with, is transformed into electrical power and in that form inserted into the power grid. There the unlocked, exposed, transformed and switched-about coal can be put to ever new uses – heat, lighting, making music (through a CD-player), providing a visual display which allows us to read books or view works of art.

As a result of all this unlocking, exposing, transforming and switching around, entities now lack any inherent significance, use or purpose. Heidegger's name for the way in which entities appear and are experienced in the technological world is 'resource' or, in the translation above, 'standing-reserve'. In the technological age, even people are reduced from modern subjects with fixed desires and a deep immanent truth, to 'functionaries of enframing' (*Bremer und Freiburger Vorträge*, p. 30). Humans in this age are driven by the desire to get the most out of their possibilities, without any real sense that any of those possibilities are inherently worthwhile. So, for example, education is increasingly aimed at providing students with 'skills' for critical thinking, writing and study, rather than at teaching students facts or training them in disciplines. This is because skills, unlike disciplines, will let students adapt to any conceivable work situation. This is driven by the need for an economy that can flexibly reconfigure itself and shift its human resources into whatever role happens to be necessary at the moment.

As we become addicted to the ease and flexibility of technological devices, we start to experience everything in terms of its ease and flexibility (or lack thereof). The result is that everything is seen, ultimately and ideally, as lacking any fixed character or determinate 'nature' or essence. This revealing 'never comes to an end', because it strives to bring everything into line as a resource, and to more effectively secure resources. We are always working, for example, to upgrade the power grid, make it more flexible, more efficient, less conspicuous, more of a resource. But the never-ending nature of technological revealing is not 'indeterminate' – everything shows up as a resource, although the precise ways we place it on call as a resource might change as technology improves.

The technologizing of everyday activities naturally changes the character of our lives in a profound and, Heidegger believes, potentially disastrous way. In particular, he writes, technology means that the entities we encounter 'no longer stand over against us as objects'. Things are no longer experienced as having inherent properties to which we need to accommodate ourselves. Dealing with objects and people that have fixed properties requires us to develop bodily and social skills, for example. Technological devices, by contrast, replace the need for bodily skills with a mechanism that does everything for us. Albert Borgmann has described, for example, how differently we think about something as commonplace as music. If one wanted to enjoy music at home in a pre-technological age, one had to develop the skills to perform music. In the technological age, one needs only to be able to click a mouse or push a button to consume music. In a technological age, therefore, we ourselves lose the skills and capacities that give us our own identity and, as importantly, we lose a kind of receptivity to the things around us. This, as we will see in the next chapter, endangers what is most essential to us as human beings.

10

OUR MORTAL DWELLING WITH THINGS

By a *primal* oneness the four – earth and sky, divinities and mortals – belong together in one.

Earth is the serving bearer, blossoming and fruiting, spreading out in rock and water, rising up into plant and animal. When we say earth, we are already thinking of the other three along with it, but we give no thought to the simple oneness of the four.

The sky is the vaulting path of the sun, the course of the changing moon, the wandering glitter of the stars, the year's seasons and their changes, the light and dusk of day, the gloom and glow of night, the clemency and inclemency of the weather, the drifting clouds and blue depth of the ether. When we say sky, we are already thinking of the other three along with it, but we give no thought to the simple oneness of the four.

The divinities are the beckoning messengers of the godhead. Out of the holy sway of the godhead, the god appears in his presence or withdraws into his concealment. When we speak of the divinities, we are already thinking of the other three along with them, but we give no thought to the simple oneness of the four.

The mortals are the human beings. They are called mortals because they can die. To die means to be capable of death *as* death. Only man dies, and indeed continually, as long as he remains on earth, under the sky, before the divinities. When we speak of mortals, we are already thinking of the other three along with them, but we give no thought to the simple oneness of the four.

This simple oneness of the four we call *the fourfold*. Mortals *are* in the fourfold by *dwelling*. But the basic character of dwelling is safeguarding. Mortals dwell in the way they preserve the fourfold in its essential being . . . Accordingly, the preserving that dwells is fourfold . . .

In saving the earth, in receiving the sky, in awaiting the divinities, in initiating mortals, dwelling occurs as the fourfold preservation of the fourfold. To spare and preserve means: to take under our care, to look after the fourfold in its essence. What we take under our care must be kept safe. But if dwelling preserves the fourfold, where does it keep the fourfold's essence? How do mortals make their dwelling such a preserving? Mortals would never be capable of it if dwelling were merely a staying on earth under the sky, before the divinities, among mortals. Rather, dwelling itself is always a staying with things. Dwelling, as preserving, keeps the fourfold in that with which mortals stay: in things.

Staying with things, however, is not merely something attached to this fourfold preserving as a fifth something. On the contrary: staying with things is the only way in which the fourfold stay within the fourfold is accomplished at any time in simple unity. Dwelling preserves the fourfold by bringing the essence of the fourfold into things. But things themselves secure the fourfold *only when* they themselves *as* things are let be in their essence. How is this done? In this way, that mortals nurse and nurture the things that grow, and specially construct things that do not grow. Cultivating and construction are building in the narrower sense. *Dwelling*, insofar as it keeps or secures the fourfold in things, is, as this keeping, *a building*. ('Building, Dwelling, Thinking', in *Poetry, Language, Thought*, pp. 149–50)

The technological understanding of being threatens to reduce everything to resources, which lack a fixed nature or intrinsic goodness and worth, and are unable to make any demands on us or require anything from us. In a technological world, we feel free to use anything in any way we please, but, correspondingly, there is no reason why we need to do anything – every thing becomes contingent and shallow, every action a meaningless expression of a whim. We ourselves end up losing our essence as technology 'strikes daily more decisively back at human being itself and degrades it to an orderable piece of resource' ('Zeichen', in *Aus der Erfahrung des Denkens*, p. 211).

From the moment that we started to exploit the awesome power of machine technology, philosophers and artists have worried about our ability to control that power. The *Matrix* movies depict in nightmarish fashion the same threat that Oswald Spengler warned about in 1931: 'The lord of the world is becoming the slave of the machine. It compels him, indeed it compels us all without exception, whether or not we know it and want it, to follow its course' (*Der Mensch und die Technik*, p. 75).

For Heidegger, by contrast, the primary worry about technology is not that we are becoming dependent on machines to supply us with the necessities of life, nor that machines hold more power to destroy life than the world has ever before seen. The real danger is that technology will deprive us of our essence as human beings: 'Human being is, according to its essence, compelled to always new experiments [on ways to be human]!' But in the technological world, 'the danger stands that man is completely delivered over to technology and one day will be made into a controlled machine' ('Aus Gesprächen mit einem buddhistischen Mönch', in *Reden*, p. 590). When we become controlled machines, we will have lost the ability of experimenting on new ways to be human. The possibility that we might become mere resources, Heidegger explained in an interview in 1969, is an even more dangerous consequence of technology than weapons of mass destruction: 'I think about what is developing today under the name of biophysics. In the foreseeable future we will be in the position to make man in a certain way, i.e. to construct him purely in his organic being according to how we need him: as fit and unfit, clever and stupid' (Wisser, p. 36). For many, of course, the prospect of biological engineering is one of the great promises still to be realized in technology. For Heidegger, it would remove the last obstacle to completely reducing us to a resource. At the point that we can create ourselves in whatever way we see fit, there will no longer be room to acknowledge any constraints on us or any demands on us that we need to respect. We will no longer encounter anything which can provoke us to find new ways to be human.

'Dwelling' is Heidegger's response to this threat. Technology creates a world within which only resources can show up; dwelling, by contrast, establishes a space in which human being can once again reclaim its essence:

> modern man must first and above all find his way back into the full breadth of the space proper to his essence . . . *Unless man first establishes himself beforehand in the space proper to his essence and there takes up his dwelling*, he will not be capable of anything essential within the destiny that now prevails. ('The Turning', p. 39, emphasis supplied, translation modified)

The word translated as 'destiny', *Geschick*, means both a skill or aptitude for something, and a fate or destiny. A destiny or fate is a setting up in advance of the way things will occur, how they will proceed. The ambiguity of the German word *Geschick* is perfect for Heidegger – it captures the way that the skills and aptitudes we have for the world both grow out of and shape the way the world itself is set up to unfold.

Technology is, in our age, our *Geschick* – our skills and dispositions are technological in nature, as is the prevailing way of unfolding things and arranging them in the world.

If we are to change our destiny, we will need to develop new skills and dispositions, and establish a space within which the world can unfold in a non-technological fashion. This is accomplished in dwelling. In dwelling, we develop practices and tastes peculiarly suited to our 'fourfold' or locale – our earth, sky, divinities, and the mortals with whom we live. We then 'preserve the fourfold in its essence' by building things peculiarly suited to our local world; 'dwelling itself is always a staying with things'. When we build such things, we no longer reduce the entities around us to mere resources. Rather, we allow them to have an essence appropriate to them. As Heidegger puts it in our passage, 'dwelling preserves the fourfold by bringing the essence of the fourfold into things. But things themselves secure the fourfold only when they themselves as things are let be in their essence.' Heidegger believes that, as we learn to live in harmony with our particular world (our earth, our sky, our mortality and our divinities), we can be pulled out of a technologically frenzied existence into a world repopulated by things and activities that really matter to us, a world where we are not ourselves merely resources to be maximized along with everything else.

In a technological world, we develop an addiction to flexibility and ease. One might think that the increased availability of everything for use in increasingly flexible ways would make our lives more thrilling, exciting and fulfilling. But Heidegger thinks that all the technological time-saving devices, meant to free us for truly worthwhile pursuits, actually lead to modern lives lived in a mood of profound boredom. This boredom gives rise to our incessant appetite for constant busyness, saturated with amusement and entertainment. Any movie or

TV show is eagerly consumed in the attempt to cover up the attunement of profound boredom that overtakes us in a world where nothing matters to us. 'For contemporary man, who no longer has time for anything, the time, if he has free time, becomes immediately too long. He must drive away the long time, in shortening it through a pastime. The amusing pastime is supposed to eliminate or at least cover up and let him forget the boredom' (*Reden*, p. 579). The boredom, Heidegger believes, is a symptom of our failure to feel at home with the technological world. The search for amusement betrays an attempt to hide our dissatisfaction with our existence, a dissatisfaction which, in turn, attests to a continued longing for home. 'Homesickness is alive there where man constantly flees into the strange, which entertains him, bewitches him, fills his time, supposedly to shorten the time, because it becomes incessantly too long for him' (*Reden*, p. 579).

To be at home somewhere means to have a way of living suited to and satisfied by a particular location or place. When it reduces everything to resources, the technological world destroys particularity in the drive towards maximal efficiency, flexibility and interchangeability. In the process, it prevents any particular thing from playing a unique and irreplaceable role in our lives: 'In enframing [i.e., the technological understanding that orders our world], everything is set up in the constant replaceability of the same through the same' (*Bremer und Freiburger Vorträge*, p. 45). Thus, whether one is in Boise, Bristol or Beijing, one can buy the same TVs at Wal-Mart or eat the same lunch at McDonald's.

Rather than increasing the universal and uniform availability of everything, we need instead to learn how to let things be things rather than resources, and develop practices attuned to the things that are peculiar to our local world with their own particular earth, sky, mortal practices and divinities.

Heidegger intends us to understand 'earth', 'sky', 'mortals' and 'divinities' in a literal fashion. The earth, here, *is* the earth beneath our feet, the earth in which plants grow, 'blossoming and fruiting', the earth that 'spreads out in rock and water', 'rises up into plant and animal'. The sky *is* the sky above our heads, 'the vaulting path of the sun, the course of the changing moon, the wandering glitter of the stars, the year's seasons and their changes, the light and dusk of day, the gloom and glow of night, the clemency and inclemency of the weather, the drifting clouds and blue depth of the ether'. The divinities are 'the beckoning messengers of divinity',[12] in other words, entities which beckon us towards or give a sign of divinity, of what is holy and beyond our power to determine or control. We *are* the mortals: 'The mortals are the human beings. They are called mortals because they can die.'

The earth, sky, mortals and divinities can become a 'simple oneness', that is, a *world*: 'World is the fourfold of earth and sky, divinities and mortals' (*Bremer und Freiburger Vorträge*, p. 48). The world is the unified and coherent whole that structures our relations to the people and things around us, even as it structures the way that things and activities line up with and refer to each other. The world opened up by the fourfold is localized and particular, having a character determined by the way that the earth, sky, mortals and divinities condition each other in our locale. They have a simple oneness because they each become what they are by, as Heidegger elsewhere says, 'mirroring' and 'ringing' or 'wrestling' with each other (see, for example, 'The Thing', p. 180). Mirroring, Heidegger explains, consists in each member of the four becoming intelligible (Heidegger's word is 'lighted') in the process of reflecting the others. I take this to mean that each member of the fourfold comes to have determinate characteristics only in so far as it comes into a particular relationship with the others. For example, the weather the sky brings is only intelligible as inclement weather given the fruits the earth tries to produce, or the activities of mortals (in my desert home, we pray for the kind of rain or snowstorms that other people might consider to be bad weather. For us, storms are experienced as a divine blessing). And the earth first comes into its essence as the earth it is when 'blossoming in the grace of the sky' (see 'Besinnung auf unser Wesen'). From out of this mutual conditioning of earth, sky, mortal practices and divinities, a world as a unified and coherent structure emerges.

We dwell by attuning our way of life to this local world: 'Mortals are in the fourfold by dwelling . . . Mortals dwell in the way they preserve the fourfold in its essence.' As Heidegger elsewhere explains, 'preserving itself does not merely consist in not doing anything to what is preserved. Genuine preserving is something positive and occurs when we leave something at rest from the outset in its essence, when we ourselves secure something back into its essence' (*Vorträge und Aufsätze*, p. 142). Rather than forcing everything to be a resource, then, we let it settle into its proper essence. Or, if it is already a resource, we 'secure or shelter it back' to its essence by developing practices that respond to it as something other than a resource. Those practices can only really take hold when they have things to deal with that are appropriate for non-technological practices. 'Things themselves secure the fourfold,' Heidegger explains, but 'only when they them- selves as things are let be in their essence'.

Let's look more closely at the idea that we can preserve the fourfold by being conditioned by it. Heidegger says that 'the preserving that dwells is fourfold', corresponding to the four dimensions of the fourfold. We dwell 'in saving the earth, in receiving the sky, in awaiting the divinities, in accompanying mortals'.[13] All of these are essentially receptive practices where our dispositions and understanding are shaped by the things with which we deal.

'Saving the earth' consists in not exploiting it, not mastering it and not subjugating it (*Vorträge und Aufsätze*, p. 143). In the desert wilderness of Utah, my home, one way to be conditioned by the earth would be to live in harmony with the desert, rather than pushing it aside (as is commonly done) by planting grass and lawns to replicate the gardens of the eastern United States (see Borgmann). The technology of modern irrigation systems and genetically modified, drought-resistant plants allows us to master the earth and subjugate it, rather than being conditioned by it. Human beings 'only experience the appropriation of the earth in the home-coming to their land', that is, when we come to be at home with our land in its *own* characteristics, not those enforced upon it (see 'Besinnung auf unser Wesen').

We receive the sky when we 'leave to the sun and the moon their journey, to the stars their courses, to the seasons their blessing and their inclemency'. Dwelling 'does not turn night into day nor day into a harassed unrest' ('Building, Dwelling, Thinking', p. 150). That means that we incorporate into our practices the temporal cycles of our heavens, the day and the night, the seasons and the weather. We push aside the sky when our eating habits demand food on call, out of season, or when our patterns of work, rest and play make no allowance for the times of day and year, or recognize no holy days or festivals.

We are conditioned by our mortality when our practices acknowledge our temporal course on earth, both growth and suffering, health and disease. We learn this by allowing our mortality to accompany or escort us into a style of life appropriate to our current strengths and capacities. Heidegger, in a letter to a friend, explained that reliance or trust in the ages of man is 'the good escort into the secret of age': 'the autumn [of life] is the superior time, which wakes the sense for the hidden harmony of all things . . . Every phase of a human life, if it is genuine, has grown into its own style' ('Theophil Rees zum sechzigsten Geburtstag', in *Reden*, p. 436). The opposite of this receptivity to mortality is to seek immediate gratification without discipline, to set aside our own local cultural practices for dealing with our age and limitations, to try to engineer biologically and pharmacologically an end to all infirmity, including even death.

We await the divinities by holding ourselves open to an encounter with something genuinely divine, expecting and hoping to be touched by the sacred. In awaiting the divinities, mortals 'wait for intimations of their coming and do not mistake the signs of their absence. They do not make their gods for themselves and do not worship idols. In evil (*Unheil*) they yet wait for the salvation (*Heils*) that has been withdrawn' ('Building, Dwelling, Thinking', p. 150; translation modified). In doing this, we will incorporate into our practices a recognition of holy times and holy precincts, perhaps manifested where one experiences the earth as God's creation, or feels a reverence for holy days or the sanctity of human life (see 'The Origin of the Work of Art', p. 167).

This fourfold way of living – saving, receiving, awaiting and escorting – can't be maintained, Heidegger argues, unless it can be a 'staying with things'. In an obvious way – perhaps so obvious that it is often overlooked – the things we use support and condition our practices and dispositions. Compare, for example, how different it would be to live in an ultramodern condominium, with radiant heat sources, electrical lighting, spectrally selective windows, etc., versus the Black Forest farmhouses of the sixteenth century. Modern housing goes out of its way to free us from the need to save the earth and sky while technologies for building, lighting and heating allow us to construct our housing in the most inhospitable places imaginable. By contrast, the Black Forest farmhouses were specifically built for the climate and terrain. Here is Heidegger's description:

> Let us think for a while of a farmhouse in the Black Forest, which was built some two hundred years ago by the dwelling of peasants. Here the self-sufficiency of the power to let earth and sky, divinities and mortals enter in simple oneness into things ordered the house. It placed the farm on the wind-sheltered mountain slope, looking south, among the meadows close to the spring. It gave it the wide overhanging shingle roof whose proper slope bears up under the burden of snow, and that, reaching deep down, shields the chambers against the storms of the long winter nights. It did not forget the altar corner behind the community table; it made room in its chamber for the hallowed places of childbed and the 'tree of the dead' – for that is what they call a coffin there: the Totenbaum – and in this way it designed for the different generations under one roof the character of their journey through time. ('Building, Dwelling, Thinking,' p. 160)

This doesn't mean, as Heidegger is quick to note, that we should build such houses. Indeed, to do so would fail to recognize our own local world. Things are 'things' in Heidegger's special sense only to the extent that we 'bring the essence of the fourfold into things' – that means, we build them 'specially', *eigens*, we do it ourselves in the light of the receptivity we have developed for our local earth, sky, mortality and divinities. If the entities we surround ourselves with have not been conditioned in this way (and resources are not), then they will not call on us to use the skills we have developed for living on the earth, beneath the sky, before the divinities. When one visits one of the few remaining original Black Forest farmhouses, one can marvel at the way they organized and shaped the lives of their inhabitants. But *we* could not live in them without considerable modification to accommodate our dietary, hygienic, familial and work practices.

Heidegger's answer to technology, then, is not nostalgic longing for 'former objects which perhaps were once on the way to becoming things and even to actually presencing as things' ('The Thing', p. 179), but rather allowing ourselves to be conditioned by our world, and then learning to 'keep the fourfold in things' by building and nurturing things peculiarly suited to our fourfold. When our practices incorporate the fourfold, our lives and everything around us will have importance far exceeding that of resources, because they and only they will be geared to our way of inhabiting the world. As a result those things only can be used to be who we are. We will thus finally be at home in our places, because our practices will be oriented to our local world alone.

In his writings on dwelling, Heidegger's thought takes a decidedly poetical turn that stands in marked contrast to the very dense and technical prose of *Being and Time* and his other early works. I think it is fair to say that most philosophers don't quite know what to do with the later Heidegger's poeticism. Nevertheless, the later works are intelligible if we understand them as a continuation of Heidegger's earlier focus on the significance of everyday practices for understanding our experience of the world.

Heidegger's account of dwelling with its emphasis on learning to be rooted in our own particular place in the world reflects Heidegger's own course in life. In his later career, Heidegger wrote often about the pastoral practices and dialect of his native region. He spent most of his career living and teaching in Freiburg, with as much time as possible in his ski hut in a rural mountain valley in Todtnauberg. Following his death in 1976, he was buried, in accordance with his wishes, in his native Messkirch. Perhaps it was no exaggeration when he claimed in 1933, having turned down a prestigious position at the University of Berlin, that his 'whole work is supported and guided by the world of these mountains and their farmers' (*Aus der Erfahrung des Denkens*, p. 11).

CHRONOLOGY

1889 Born on 26 September in Messkirch, Germany.

1903–9 Attends gymnasium in Constance and Freiburg.

1909 Candidate for novitiate with Jesuits near Feldkirch, Austria. Discharged after two weeks because of health problems.

1909–13 Studies first theology and mathematics, and then philosophy at Freiburg University.

1913 Receives his doctorate of philosophy from Freiburg University with a thesis on 'The Doctrine of Judgment in Psychologism' (*Die Lehre vom Urteil im Psychologismus*).

1915 Becomes a lecturer (*Dozent*) at Freiburg University with the completion of his dissertation entitled 'The Doctrine of Categories and Meaning in Duns Scotus' (*Die Kategorien- und Bedeutungslehre des Duns Scotus*).

1915–18 Military service.

1917 Marries Elfride Petri.

1919 Writes to Father Engelbert Krebs that his 'inner calling to philosophy' leads him to reject the 'system of Catholicism'.

1919–23 Lectures on phenomenology at Freiburg University; works as assistant to Edmund Husserl.

1923 Receives appointment as Associate Professor of Philosophy at Marburg University.

1924 Beginning of a love affair with Hannah Arendt.

1927 Publication of *Being and Time* (*Sein und Zeit*).

1928 Succeeds Husserl as Professor of Philosophy at the University of Freiburg.

1933 Joins the National Socialist Party and is elected rector of Freiburg University.

1934 Resigns as rector.

1935–6 Lectures in Freiburg, Zürich and Frankfurt on 'The Origin of the Work of Art'.

1936–40 Lectures on Nietzsche.

1944 Drafted into the People's Militia (*Volkssturm*)

1945 Hearings before the Denazification Committee.

1946–9 Banned from university teaching.

1949 Lectures in Bremen on 'The Thing', 'Enframing', 'The Danger' and 'The Turning'.

1951–2 Heidegger reinstated to his teaching position; lectures at Freiburg University on 'What is Called Thinking?' (*Was heisst Denken?*).

1951 Lectures in Darmstadt on 'Building, Dwelling, Thinking'.

1955 Lectures in Munich on 'The Question Concerning Technology'.

1959 Publication of 'On the Way to Language' (*Unterwegs zur Sprache*).

1976 Dies in Freiburg, Germany, on 26 May.

1976 Buried in Messkirch, Germany, on 28 May.

NOTES

1 See, for example, *Existence and Being*.

2 In fact, the German verb Heidegger is using, *sich verhalten*, is ambiguous, and can mean either a relation to something (*sich verhalten zu . . .*), or a way of acting or carrying or comporting oneself (*sich verhalten gegenüber* or *sich verhalten mit*). A more natural translation of the opening sentence of our passage would be: 'Dasein is a being which, in understanding its being, relates to this being.' But Heidegger believes that all our authentic relationships grow out of the ability to comport or conduct ourselves in the proper way vis-à-vis the object to which we relate: 'the relation to (*das Verhalten zu . . .*) . . . is authentic precisely when it is originally and only comportment (*Verhalten*)' or, in other words, 'the genuinely meaningful relation to . . . arises as a pure execution from out of an independent comportment'. *Phänomenologische Interpretationen zu Aristoteles*, p. 52. For Heidegger's discussion of the productive ambiguity of the German term '*Verhalten*', see ibid. pp. 51–3.

3 Heidegger objected, however, to Sartre's way of thinking about the relationship between existence and essence. Heidegger thought that Sartre was too ready to think of man's existence in the same way as he thought of the substantiality of other things, while Heidegger himself saw existence as opening us up to possibilities for reinterpreting ourselves that substantial things don't have. See Heidegger, 'Letter on Humanism'.

4 The translation 'state-of-mind' is misleading because it gives the impression that our way of finding ourselves in the world is something mental or merely 'in our minds'. But nothing could be further from Heidegger's intention: *Befindlichkeit* comes from the verb *befinden*, literally, to be found (the root word *finden* means 'to find'). Thus the adjective *befindlich* is used when something exists, when it is 'findable' in the world. From this literal sense, the verb

befinden can also be used to refer to the condition or state that one finds oneself in. To capture all of these senses, the best English translation of *Befindlichkeit* is probably 'disposedness', as this contains both the notion of the disposition of entities in the world (the way they are found to be), and the condition or disposition that I have with respect to those entities (I find myself well-disposed or poorly disposed towards them, for instance). I will thus substitute 'disposedness' for the phrase 'state-of-mind'.

5 Of course, we all recognize that moods can at times distort our experience of a situation – one need think only of Othello's tragic submission to his jealousy. But this doesn't show that we should free ourselves from all moods. Instead, it shows that there are right and wrong moods for coping with a situation. Othello should have been suspicious of Iago.

6 To show that they are identical, we would need to show that the only way to existentially die is to demise. But Heidegger seems to think that this is not the case – that we may lose our ability to be in the world, even if we don't suffer a physical death.

7 After noting that death is 'a possibility of Dasein's being', Heidegger observes that 'to concern oneself with actualizing what is thus possible would have to signify, "bringing about one's demise"' (*Being and Time*, p. 305). Demise, in other words, is one way to actualize the possibility of death, which means, to make it impossible to exist in the world. This is why Heidegger believes that 'medical and biological investigation into "demising" can obtain results which may even become significant ontologically if the basic orientation for an existential interpretation of death has been made secure' (*Being and Time*, p. 291).

8 My demise is one kind of event that could produce this failure, that is, making it impossible to continue being in my world. The collapse of my world might be another.

9 Interestingly enough, it is not at all obvious that the move to modernize Japan should have been motivated by a desire to improve the physical well-being of the Japanese people in general. There is no necessary correlation between average or per capita income and things like health, literacy and life expectancy. As Susan B. Hanley has persuasively argued, the physical well-being of the Japanese prior to modernization was at least on a par, if not in some respects (like literacy) actually higher than, that of their counterparts in industrialized countries: 'The level of physical

well-being [of the Japanese] was at least as high as that in England in the nineteenth century, at a time when Japan had not yet begun to industrialize and England was already an industrial nation.' *Everyday Things in Premodern Japan: The Hidden Legacy of Material Culture* (Berkeley: University of California Press, 1997), p. 13. The Japanese were able to exceed Western standards of well-being even without the productivity that modernization brought because the style of their culture promoted resource-efficiency, hygiene and health in housing and diet, and a minimalist sense of luxury. 'The result was that the population achieved a higher level of physical well-being using fewer resources and with the need for less income than was required in the West for the same level of physical well-being' (ibid., p. 22).

10 The published translation of this essay has inexplicably translated Heidegger's term '*Sprachwesen*' simply as 'language'.

11 In the excerpt above, this phrase reads 'the maximum yield at the minimum expense'. This is a misleading translation, because it sounds as if there is some fixed 'yield' that we are always after – yielding the greatest wealth, or something like that. 'Yield' is a permissible translation of the German '*Nutzung*', but a more literal translation captures more clearly what Heidegger is trying to say. '*Nutzen*' is the verb 'to make use of', so a '*Nutzung*' is a use. Our technological practices are directed, then, not at the greatest yield, but at 'the greatest possible use'.

12 I've altered the translation. The word *Gottheit* means literally God-ness, godhead in the sense of the divine essence, i.e., divinity. It shouldn't be heard as referring to any specific god.

13 I've altered the translation again. *Geleiten* doesn't mean to initiate something, it means to escort or accompany it.

REFERENCES

Ayer, A. J., 'One's Knowledge of Other Minds' in *Essays in Philosophical Psychology*, ed. Donald F. Gustafson (Garden City, New York: Anchor Books, 1964), pp. 346–76.

Borgmann, Albert, *Technology and the Character of Contemporary Life* (Chicago: University of Chicago Press, 1987).

Brock, Werner, *An Introduction to Contemporary German Philosophy* (Cambridge: Cambridge University Press, 1935).

Descartes, René, *Discourse on Method and Meditations on First Philosophy*, trans. Donald A. Cress (Hackett, 1980).

Dreyfus, Hubert, 'Heidegger's Ontology of Art,' in *A Companion to Heidegger*, eds. Hubert Dreyfus and Mark Wrathall (Oxford: Blackwell, 2005).

Dummett, Michael, *Origins of Analytical Philosophy* (Cambridge, MA: Harvard University Press, 1994).

Glicksman, Marjorie, 'A Note on the Philosophy of Heidegger', *Journal of Philosophy*, 35:4 (1938), 93–104.

Grimm, Jacob, and Grimm, Wilhelm, *Deutsches Wörterbuch*, vol. 1 (Munich: Deutscher Taschenbuch Verlag, 1999).

Hanley, Susan B., *Everyday Things in Premodern Japan: The Hidden Legacy of Material Culture* (Berkeley: University of California Press, 1997).

Heidegger, Martin, *Aus der Erfahrung des Denkens. Gesamtausgabe*, vol. 13 (Frankfurt: Vittorio Klostermann, 1983).

— *The Basic Problems of Phenomenology*, trans. A. Hofstadter (Bloomington: Indiana University Press, 1982).

— *Basic Questions of Philosophy: Selected "Problems" of "Logic"*, trans. Richard Rojcewicz and André Schuwer (Bloomington: Indiana University Press, 1994).

— *Basic Writings*, rev. edn., various translators, ed. David Farrell Krell (San Francisco: HarperSanFrancisco, 1993).

— *Being and Time*, trans. J. Macquarrie and E. Robinson (San

Francisco: HarperSanFrancisco, 1962).
— *Beiträge zur Philosophie (Vom Ereignis). Gesamtausgabe*, vol. 65 (Frankfurt: Vittorio Klostermann, 1989).
— 'Besinnung auf unser Wesen', ed. F. W. von Herrmann (Frankfurt am Main: Private Publication of the Martin Heidegger Gesellschaft, 1994).
— *Bremer und Freiburger Vorträge. Gesamtausgabe*, vol. 79 (Frankfurt: Vittorio Klostermann, 1994).
— *Einführung in die phänomenologische Forschung. Gesamtausgabe*, vol. 17 (Frankfurt: Vittorio Klostermann, 1994).
— *Einleitung in die Philosophie. Gesamtausgabe*, vol. 27 (Frankfurt: Vittorio Klostermann, 1996).
— *Existence and Being*, trans. Werner Brock (Chicago: H. Regnery, 1949).
— *Frühe Schriften. Gesamtausgabe*, vol. 1 (Frankfurt: Vittorio Klostermann, 1978).
— *History of the Concept of Time: Prolegomena*, trans. T. Kisiel (Bloomington: Indiana University Press, 1985).
— *Hölderlins Hymnen 'Germanien' und 'Der Rhein'. Gesamtausgabe*, vol. 39 (Frankfurt: Vittorio Klostermann, 1980).
— *Holzwege. Gesamtausgabe*, vol. 5 (Frankfurt: Vittorio Klostermann, 1977).
— 'Language', in *Poetry, Language, Thought*.
— 'Letter on Humanism', in *Pathmarks*, ed. William McNeill (Cambridge: Cambridge University Press, 1998).
— *Logik als die Frage nach dem Wesen der Sprache. Gesamtausgabe*, vol. 38 (Frankfurt: Vittorio Klostermann, 1998).
— 'The Nature of Language', in *On the Way to Language*.
— *On the Way to Language*, trans. Peter D. Hertz and Joan Stambaugh (San Francisco: HarperSanFrancisco, 1982).
— 'Only a God Can Save Us: *Der Spiegel*'s interview with Martin Heidegger', in *The Heidegger Controversy: A Critical Reader*, ed. Richard Wolin (Cambridge: MIT Press, 1993).
— 'The Origin of the Work of Art', in *Basic Writings*, rev. edn., various translators, ed. David Krell (San Francisco: HarperSanFrancisco, 1993).
— *Phänomenologische Interpretationen zu Aristoteles. Gesamtausgabe*, vol. 61 (Frankfurt: Vittorio Klostermann, 1985).
— *Plato's Sophist*, trans. R. Rojcewicz and A. Schuwer (Bloomington: Indiana University Press, 1997).

— *Poetry, Language, Thought*, trans. A. Hofstadter (New York: HarperCollins, 2001).

— *Prolegomena zur Geschichte des Zeitbegriffs. Gesamtausgabe*, vol. 20 (Frankfurt: Vittorio Klostermann, 1979).

— *The Question Concerning Technology and Other Essays*, trans. W. Lovitt (New York: Harper & Row, 1977).

— *Reden. Gesamtausgabe*, vol. 16 (Frankfurt: Vittorio Klostermann, 2000).

— *Seminare. Gesamtausgabe*, vol. 15 (Frankfurt: Vittorio Klostermann, 1986).

— *Supplements*, trans. John van Buren (Albany: SUNY Press, 2002).

— 'The Thing', in *Poetry, Language, Thought*.

— *Unterwegs zur Sprache. Gesamtausgabe*, vol. 12 (Frankfurt: Vittorio Klostermann, 1985).

— *Vorträge und Aufsätze. Gesamtausgabe*, vol. 7 (Frankfurt: Vittorio Klostermann, 2000).

— *Was heisst Denken? Gesamtausgabe*, vol. 8 (Frankfurt: Vittorio Klostermann, 2002).

— *Wegmarken. Gesamtausgabe*, vol. 9 (Frankfurt: Vittorio Klostermann, 1976).

Kierkegaard, Søren, *Concluding Unscientific Postscript*, vol. 1, trans. Howard V. Hong and Edna H. Hong (Princeton: Princeton University Press, 1992).

Long, A. A. and Sedley, D. N. (eds), *The Hellenistic Philosophers*, vol. 1 (Cambridge: Cambridge University Press, 1987).

Mackie, J. L., *Ethics: Inventing Right and Wrong* (London: Penguin Books, 1977).

Searle, John R., 'The Limits of Phenomenology', in *Heidegger, Coping, and Cognitive Science*, eds. Mark Wrathall and Jeff Malpas (Cambridge: MIT Press, 2000).

Spengler, Oswald, *Der Mensch und die Technik* (Munich: C. H. Beck, 1931).

Spindler, Konrad, *The Man in the Ice* (New York: Harmony, 1994).

Thomson, Iain, *Heidegger on Ontotheology: Technology and the Politics of Education* (New York: Cambridge University Press, 2005).

Thomson, Iain, 'Heidegger and National Socialism', in *A Companion to Heidegger*, eds. Hubert Dreyfus and Mark Wrathall (Oxford: Blackwell, 2005).

Wilde, Oscar, *De Profundis* (New York: Vintage Books, 1964).

Wisser, Richard, *Martin Heidegger in Conversation* (New Delhi: Arnold-Heinemann, 1977).

SUGGESTIONS FOR FURTHER READING

Biographies

Ott, Hugo, *Martin Heidegger: A Political Life*, trans. Allan Blunden (Basic Books, 1993).

Safranski, Rüdiger, *Martin Heidegger: Between Good and Evil*, trans. Ewald Osers (Harvard University Press, 1999).

On *Being and Time*

Dreyfus, Hubert, *Being-in-the-World: A Commentary on Heidegger's* Being and Time, *Division I* (MIT Press, 1990).

Mulhall, Stephen, *Heidegger and* Being and Time (Routledge, 1996).

Blattner, William, *Heidegger's Temporal Idealism* (Cambridge University Press, 1999).

Carman, Taylor, *Heidegger's Analytic: Interpretation, Discourse, and Authenticity in* Being and Time (Cambridge University Press, 2003).

Kisiel, Theodore, *The Genesis of Heidegger's* Being and Time (University of California Press, 1995).

Heidegger's involvement with National Socialism

Neske, Günther, and Kettering, Emil (eds), *Martin Heidegger and National Socialism: Questions and Answers*, trans. L. Harries (Paragon House, 1990).

Wolin, Richard (ed.), *The Heidegger Controversy* (MIT Press, 1993).

Sluga, Hans, *Heidegger's Crisis* (Harvard University Press, 1993).

General anthologies on Heidegger's work

Guignon, Charles (ed.), *The Cambridge Companion to Heidegger*, rev. edn. (Cambridge University Press, 2005).

Dreyfus, Hubert, and Wrathall, Mark (eds.), *A Companion to Heidegger* (Blackwell, 2005).

Dreyfus, Hubert, and Wrathall, Mark (eds.), *Heidegger Reexamined* (Routledge, 2002).
> Volume One: *Dasein, Authenticity, and Death*
> Volume Two: *Truth, Realism, and the History of Being*
> Volume Three: *Art, Poetry, and Technology*
> Volume Four: *Language and the Critique of Subjectivity*

Faulconer, James, and Wrathall, Mark (eds.), *Appropriating Heidegger* (Cambridge University Press, 2000).

Wrathall, Mark, and Malpas, Jeff (eds.), *Heidegger, Authenticity, and Modernity* (Cambridge: MIT Press, 2000).

Wrathall, Mark, and Malpas, Jeff (eds.), *Heidegger, Coping and Cognitive Science* (Cambridge: MIT Press, 2000).

On Heidegger's later philosophy

Thomson, Iain, *Heidegger on Ontotheology* (New York: Cambridge University Press, 2005).

Young, Julian, *Heidegger's Later Philosophy* (Cambridge University Press, 2001).

INTERNET RESOURCES

A very thorough lexicon of *Sein und Zeit* (*Being and Time*), with some useful background material can be found at *www.philosophisches-lesen.de/heidegger/suz/uebersicht.html*

A wide variety of information and links concerning Heidegger's life and work can be found at *www.webcom.com/~paf/ereignis.html* and in German at: *www.heidegger.org*

Guides to Internet resources on Martin Heidegger can be found at *www.martin-heidegger.org* and *www.epistemelinks.com/Main/Philosophers.aspx?PhilCode=Heid*

Information on the collected writings of Martin Heidegger can be found at *www.klostermann.de* and on English translations of Heidegger's work at *http://think.hyperjeff.net/Heidegger/english.html*

Bibliographic information on Heidegger is available through a website maintained by the University of Freiburg at *www.ub.uni-freiburg.de/referate/02/heidegger/heidgg00.html*

Heidegger's collected papers are archived at the German Literature Archive in Marbach, Germany (*Deutsches Literaturarchiv Marbach*). Information on the archive's holdings can be found at *www.dla-marbach.de/kallias/hyperkuss/h-41.html*

Heidegger's hometown of Messkirch, Germany, maintains a website with information on the Martin Heidegger Museum at *www.messkirch.de*

In 'The Origin of the Work of Art', Heidegger discusses several works of art. Pictures of the ancient Greek temples of Paestum can be viewed at *www.paestum.org/galleria_fotografica/welcome.htm*

Links to Van Gogh's paintings titled *A Pair of Shoes* (there are many paintings with the same title) can be found at *www.vangoghgallery.com/painting/main_pr.htm*

For a virtual tour of the Black Forest farmhouses that Heidegger discusses in 'Building Dwelling Thinking', visit the website of the

Black Forest Open-Air Museum Vogtsbauernhof (*Schwarzwälder Freilichtmuseum Vogtsbauernhof*) at *www.vogtsbauernhof.org*

To see a demonstration of Heidegger's claim that technology orders everything as a resource, flexibly and efficiently available for use, visit any of the links above.

INDEX

values 19
Van Gogh, Vincent: *A Pair of Shoes*
    71, 74–5

Weber, Max 100
Western culture 101
wherein 18, 28
Wilde, Oscar 50, 56
windmills 98, 103
with-which 17, 27
world
    and earth 82–3
    establishing a new 80–81
    feeling for foreign worlds 20

freedom from 32
modern scientific study of 18
risk of overlooking it 28–9
role of 75–6, 112
structure 28
submission to 32, 34–5
succession of different worlds
    100–101
that wherein all of our actions
    make sense 28
as that in which we find ourselves
    27
as the "wherein" of an active
    understanding 28

22. Jan. 08   Amazon   9.56   104122